DISCONTINUITY & HOPE

---- ❧ ----

Radical Change and the Path to the Future

LYLE E. SCHALLER

ABINGDON PRESS
Nashville

DISCONTINUITY AND HOPE:
RADICAL CHANGE AND THE PATH TO THE FUTURE

Copyright © 1999 by Abingdon Press

All rights reserved.

Interior design J. S. Lofbomm

This book is printed on elemental-chlorine–free paper.

Library of Congress Cataloging-in-Publication Data

Schaller, Lyle E.
    Discontinuity & hope: radical change and the path to the future/
Lyle E. Schaller.
      p. cm.
Includes bibliographical references.
ISBN 0-687-08539-X (pbk.: alk. paper)
    1. Church management—United States.   2. United States—Church
history—20th century. I. Title.
BV652.S292   1999
250'.973'01—dc21

                                       98-30482
                                         CIP

00 01 02 03 04 05 06 07 08 — 10 9 8 7 6 5 4 3 2

MANUFACTURED IN THE UNITED STATES OF AMERICA

To
Walter & Tillie, Mrs. Powell, Rex, Philip Sedgwick,
Genevieve and Daisy, Herb, Cefford and Raymond,
P. M. Willis, Mr. & Mrs. A.T.P., Phyllis & Porter Clinton,
Elizabeth & Jose, Arthur & Marianna,
John & Grace, Cowboy Bill, Mushy Gush,
Walter K. Johnson, Ivan Nestingen,
Fred H. Harrington, Joost to Suder to Fain, Petunia, Fred,
Bob & Dave, Paul Pettit, Bill & Charlotte, Wayne Clymer,
Mary Worth, Sam Emerich, Dusty, Gene & Marilyn,
Shang, Peanuts, Dan O'Connell, Hemingway, Bob Burt,
Cady, Stephen Baldwin,
Jacob, Calvin & Hobbes, Clara & Nicholas, Dilbert,
Henry, Jimmy Jackson, Forty Second- & Third-Grade
Cyclists in Tibet, Several SWA Flight Attendants

CONTENTS

Introduction

─────────── ❧ ───────────

Back in the early years of the twentieth century, thousands of congregations all across the North maintained two large buildings on their property. One was a large building in which people gathered for worship, learning, inspiration, and fellowship. The other was a long, low, one-story structure, often open on the south. It sheltered the horses that brought people to church. Most of these horse sheds were razed in the 1915–22 era as the automobile replaced the horse. Thirty years later the paved parking lot began to appear on many church sites.

In the early 1960s the number of television sets in private households exceeded the number of households. Thirty-five years later the use of projected visual imagery to illustrate sermons began to become widespread in the churches.

Regional shopping malls began to appear in large numbers in the 1956–62 era. Thirty years later a growing number of congregational leaders recognized the need to redefine the role of their congregation as a regional church, rather than attempt to perpetuate the old role as a neighborhood parish.

The concept of multiple sites for department stores, financial institutions, universities, public libraries, theological schools, medical clinics, law firms, and hospitals surfaced during the 1950s but did not become popular until the 1960s. Thirty years later a small but growing number of

Protestant congregations have accepted a role as a multisite church.

The Nineteenth Amendment to the United States Constitution took effect on August 26, 1920. Thirty-five years later several religious traditions began to ordain women.

Radio introduced the concept that the hour is divided into four segments of fifteen minutes each. By 1968 television had begun to persuade viewers that an hour should be divided into two thirty-minute segments. Thirty years later many churches still begin worship services, classes, or meetings on the quarter hour.

By 1975 one-half of all housing units in the United States enjoyed room or central air-conditioning. Thirty years later it will be rare to find a church building without any air-conditioning.

In 1946, for the first time in American history, the number of divorces in the United States exceeded 600,000 (compared to 236,000 ten years earlier and 264,000 in 1940). Thirty years later, divorced ministers were being called or appointed or elected as parish pastors and as denominational executives in significant numbers.

These eight examples introduce the three central themes of this book. The first is the conviction that while there was considerable continuity in American Christianity between 1800 and 1960, the past four decades of Christianity in America have been marked by an unprecedented degree of discontinuity. That is close to an objective fact.

The second theme is more subjective. While it is both intellectually and spiritually stimulating, as well as threatening, to talk about change and discontinuity with the past, it is far more productive to focus on the consequences of this change and discontinuity. The identification and description of the probable consequences clearly is a speculative undertaking. That explains why approximately one-half of the sentences in this book focus on the consequences of change. Three of the most significant and overlapping consequences discussed repeatedly in this volume are: (1) it is far more challenging, difficult, and satisfying to be an effective parish pastor today than it was in the 1950s; (2) the competition among the churches for future constituencies is without precedent in American Christianity; and (3) for many the most threatening consequence is the emergence of the very large regional church, while for others that is one of the most hopeful developments. Any one of those three statements can be written at the top of a piece of paper and the other two listed below it as consequences.

The third theme is the most subjective of the three. This is the conviction that most of the consequences of discontinuity are turning out to be signs of hope for the future of the Christian churches in America.

One common price tag on hope is that life becomes more complex than it was earlier. One reason for this increased complexity is that there is an increased number of points of discontinuity with the past. A second reason is that the degree of discontinuity is greater today than in earlier decades. A third is the disruptive impact of several overlapping changes. Another reason is that for many adults their church has become the number one stability zone in their life. Thus when change comes to the church, it can be especially threatening.

A fifth part of the explanation for that increased level of complexity is that the normal, natural, and predictable response to discontinuity is denial. That stage of denial often endures for at least one generation and usually is accompanied by confusion, gloom, conflict, attempts to perpetuate yesterday, bewilderment, confrontations, pessimism, and sometimes even chaos, but rarely by support for creativity.

For many adults the local high school is an outstanding symbol of discontinuity with "how it used to be."

The number of juniors and seniors in a suburban Chicago public school who come to classes in their own motor vehicle is more than ten times what it was when the present buildings were constructed. That is a point of great discontinuity with the past and an objective fact. The school has plenty of classrooms but a shortage of parking. That also is an objective fact. The school district also provides buses to transport students to school at no direct charge to the student. The design of the bus route requires seniors to ride on the same buses as ninth and tenth graders. Is that good or bad? That depends on your values, your goals, and your criteria for evaluation. One senior evaluated it as comparable to "having your mother walk you to school in the morning and come after school to walk you home."

One consequence is that hundreds of students pay $60 to $80 a month for their own parking space on private property near the school. Many students have at least six choices: (1) walk; (2) ride the bus; (3) drive and pay for parking; (4) arrive ninety minutes before classes to secure a free parking space on the street; (5) ride with a fellow student; or (6) have their parents transport them to and from school. Is that array of choices a cause for despair or a reason for rejoicing? That depends on your values, your goals, and your criteria for evaluation. The parents may come to a different conclusion than their teenage children.

A neighbor who owns a home with a wide driveway across the street from the high school is unhappy with the increased volume of traffic but concedes, "That $4,000 a year from renting six parking spaces in my driveway does help pay the taxes."

The reader of this book also has choices. One is to dispute the factual basis used to identify these points of discontinuity with the past. A second is to accept as accurate the identification of the sources of discontinuity—and perhaps add a few that were omitted—but redefine the probable consequences. A third choice is to view these consequences as sources of despair and gloom. A fourth choice is to perceive many of them as signs of hope and use these as foundations for designing ministry with new generations in the twenty-first century. A fifth is to buy this book but not read it. (A sixth, regrettably, is to borrow a copy of this book. Abingdon Press prefers readers purchase books.)

How will the clergy respond to this book? Nearly all will agree that being an effective parish pastor is far more difficult today than it was forty years ago. Some, and hopefully most, also will agree that this is one reason why the pastoral ministry is both more challenging and professionally more satisfying than ever before. At least a few may explain that this is why the crucial question in evaluating a ministerial pension system is whether it facilitates early retirement.

How will the clergy respond to this book? That will be influenced by their values, goals, and criteria for evaluation. Those who are driven by a powerful future-oriented view and who enjoy new opportunities for innovation, creativity, and outreach probably will be encouraged by the discussions on consequences. Those who are more comfortable with placing tradition on a par with Scripture as a source of authority may be more comfortable either (a) engaging in denial or (b) refuting most of the points of discontinuity and the probable consequences.

When confronted with an overwhelming degree of complexity, all of us normal people attempt to break it down into manageable pieces that we can comprehend on a one-at-a-time basis. That is one reason for a mother to give birth to five babies, one at a time, over ten or twelve years rather than to bring quintuplets home from the hospital. That explains why a congregation would be well advised not to swap pastors in the middle of a building program. That also explains the outline of this book. Don't overload the system!

The first chapter discusses a dozen points of discontinuity

with the past that have emerged within the larger context of American Christianity. The first six are placed first because they represent big surprises to those of us who carry powerful firsthand memories from the 1950s.

The second chapter shifts the focus to the larger stage of American culture and identifies seven points of discontinuity that have had an immense impact on the churches. It is worth mentioning that five of these were largely the product of governmental initiatives.

The lengthy third chapter is so long because the generations born after 1940 have radically altered the context for doing ministry. Before these generations grew into adolescence the churches could say, "This is our agenda, take it or leave it." These folks brought their own agenda and proclaimed, "This is our agenda. Listen or we'll leave and go elsewhere." One symbol of that confrontation was the call for self-determination. A second was a new era of Christian music. One consequence has been an increase in the number of church buildings occupied by a shrinking number of mature adults. Another has been a flood of new nondenominational regional congregations. Eighteen items on the agendas brought by these younger generations are discussed in the third chapter.

The fourth chapter reviews seven other points of discontinuity that have been widely ignored and do not fit neatly in any of the other three categories. (At this point a few old friends may note that 12 plus 7 plus 18 plus 7 adds up to 44, but that is simply a coincidence!)

Finally, the last chapter represents an attempt to look at consequences from the perspective of those who will be affected rather than from the perspective of the causes. It may turn out that the most radical consequences will be felt by those organizations and processes designed to prepare the next generation of parish pastors and program staff for ministry in the very large regional churches. That last chapter concludes with a brief discussion of several signs of hope for the future.

For those literary genealogists who are curious about the ancestry of this volume, it is a grandchild of *It's a Different World* published in 1987. That book, which was written near the end of what now appears to be a long and clearly defined era, was an attempt to look back and explain the impact of the changes that were being felt by pastors, congregations, and denominational systems.

This book is being written from the perspective of what appears to be ten or twelve years into a completely new and radically different era in the history of American Christianity. The focus here is to look ahead to the probable consequences of radical and widespread discontinuity with the past. That earlier book was about the "what" of change. This is more about the "why" of change. The hope is that considerable grief, disappointment, and counterproductive behavior can be eliminated if specific policy statements and decisions are made from within a larger context. Ideally, someone in that policy-making group will keep raising the question, "What are the probable future consequences if we do that and if it works?" That is a far better question than "How can we perpetuate yesterday for at least a few more years?"

A few readers may ask what is the difference between this book and four earlier books I have written on planned change. That is an excellent question! The central difference can be seen most clearly when planned change is contrasted with radical discontinuity. Carefully designed and well-executed strategies for change usually produce anticipated results plus a modest number of unanticipated surprises. By contrast, radical discontinuity normally is followed by a large number of unanticipated and often disruptive surprises plus a more modest number of anticipated consequences.

One lesson from that paragraph is this. If you are designing a strategy for planned change that includes considerable continuity with the past—and that usually is the wisest approach to planned change—spend part of the time seeking to identify the probable consequences of those proposed changes. If, however, the design calls for a substantial degree of discontinuity with the past, the prudent leaders will invest more resources in that effort to anticipate the consequences. That investment usually can reduce the level of disruption created by implementation of the strategy.

One point of commonality in these two books, published a dozen years apart, is the conviction that it is much more difficult to be an effective parish pastor today than it was in the 1950s and earlier—but today it also is much more challenging and rewarding.[1]

The second point of commonality is that in both books I have attempted to inject a note of hope wherever it is appropriate. The big difference is that I am more convinced today than I was a dozen years ago that discontinuity with the past often is a powerful source of hope for new generations, even when that discontinuity is a cause for alarm among the leaders in old institutions.

Finally, this book is dedicated to a number of folks who have made life's journey far more fun and interesting than it would have been without them. Many of them really do exist, several are still alive, and all have enriched my life.

1
CONTINUITY TO DISCONTINUITY

"What's the biggest single change you have seen in the parish ministry since you were a pastor back in the 1950s?" That is a question I have been asked to address on many occasions. For several years I evaded the point of the question and came up with an excessively long list.

The Dumb Answer

1. The challenge to be an effective parish pastor is far more demanding and difficult today than it was forty years ago.

2. The high level of competition among the churches to reach potential future members is without precedent in American church history.

3. While it may not be the most significant, the greatest single point of recent discontinuity with the past is the current openness in tens of thousands of churches to a pastor who has been divorced and remarried and continues in the parish ministry.

4. Perhaps the most influential change has been the rebirth of an emphasis on evangelism and the acceptance of the lessons of the church growth movement among many denominations and congregations on the left half of the theological spectrum.

5. From the perspective of millions of individual Christians, the most significant change has been the emergence of the contemporary small-group movement.

6. From the preachers' perspective, the emergence of television has transformed worship, preaching, and learning to a degree never dreamed of in the radio world of the 1930s and 1940s.

7. The erosion of inherited institutional and denominational loyalties and the growing distrust of big bureaucratic organizations[1] has transformed the relationships between congregations and the local leadership on the one hand and denominational systems on the other hand. The basic pattern in the larger Protestant denominations has been an increasing degree of alienation between congregations and national headquarters and a growing sense of a partnership in ministry between congregations and their regional judicatories or simply within a cluster of congregations.

8. For many the most comforting change is the flood of people who dropped out of church in the 1960s and who are now heavily involved in the life and ministries of worshiping communities. (This response is especially common among old men who perceive anyone born after 1945 to be young.)

9. The growing emphasis on (a) the importance of interpersonal relationships and (b) specialized roles over functional skills and a role as a generalist in ministry is the most subtle change in staffing larger congregations.

10. The emergence of the large regional church as the successor to the traditional neighborhood congregation must be high on this list. In terms of the impact on the role of the laity, on the vocational plans of the clergy, on the priorities of denominational systems, on the mission of theological schools, and on the expectations younger generations bring to church, this change, as is suggested in the next chapter, may be the most significant of all.

When challenged to respond to the question by isolating

the single most significant change, I usually declared it was a toss-up between the first and last two of those ten.

After several years of weaseling on that question, I finally concluded I was offering a dumb answer to a bad question.

A better answer to that question would be, "Between 1958 and 1998, Christian churchgoers and congregational and denominational leaders in North America have experienced an unprecedented degree of discontinuity with the past."

In television terms this book has three overlapping story lines. One is the many points of discontinuity with the past. The second is the consequences of that discontinuity with the past. The third is the conviction that the best is yet to come.

That statement creates a three-part conceptual framework for reflecting on change. The first part of that larger conceptual framework is to identify some of the most significant points of discontinuity on the ecclesiastical scene. The second part calls for identifying the major points of discontinuity with the past in the secular or cultural context for ministry. Several of those are discussed in the next three chapters. The third and overlapping component of that three-part conceptual framework examines some of the consequences of that discontinuity with the past from six different perspectives.

Thus the fact that the call to be an effective parish pastor today is far more demanding and difficult—and often more rewarding—than it was in the 1950s is a consequence of the combination of several points of discontinuity with the past. Likewise the increased competition among the churches for potential future members is not simply a change, it is a result or product of many changes. That three-part framework for reflecting on change has become the central organizing principle for this book.

It is extremely difficult to draw a line between causes and

consequences, so the two are combined in these first four chapters. A second subjective issue is how many major points of discontinuity a reader can tolerate. Since twelve is a good biblical number, that is the answer to that second question for this chapter. A third subjective question is where to begin. The decision for this book was to begin with the ecclesiastical environment and subsequently move on to a review of the changing secular context for ministry.

Six Big Surprises

Finally, instead of beginning by attempting to identify the greatest point of discontinuity with the past, this discussion will begin with a different question. What have been the greatest surprises? If a knowledgeable Christian leader in the United States had gone to sleep in 1958 and awakened forty years later, what would that contemporary Rip Van Winkle point to as the most surprising points of discontinuity on the religious scene since the 1950s? From this observer's perspective, six stand out as surprises to the leaders of the 1950s who had been born in the 1880–1930 era. These may not be the six most important changes, but each represents a tremendous degree of discontinuity with the pre-1950 era.

The Ecumenical Movement

As Methodist pastors in Wisconsin in the 1950s, many of us identified ourselves by a one-word designation, "non-Lutheran–Protestant." In a state where approximately four out of five Anglo churchgoers were either Roman Catholic or Lutheran, it was tempting to identify ourselves by who we were not. Similarly many Republicans of that era identified themselves as not being in sympathy with Senator Joe McCarthy. Leaders with a long memory can recall the celebration of Reformation Sunday in many congregations in the 1950s. That was one way we identified ourselves by who we were not.

While this has been more pronounced in the United States than in Canada, North American Christians frequently have lifted up the differences that divide when describing the lines of demarcation that separated one religious tradition from another. Kent Hunter has described this in terms of the consequences that followed the shipwreck that landed a hundred Lutherans on a desert island. What did they do? They built two churches, one to attend and one to stay away from.

This definition of lines of demarcation was and is a widely used conceptual framework all across our culture. Rural America was divided between "rural" and "rural nonfarm." Eventually "nonmetropolitan" became a synonym for "rural." For several decades the Norwegian Lutheran parish found it easy to explain why it was affiliated with a different Lutheran denomination than the German Lutheran church meeting in a building two blocks to the east or the Swedish Lutheran church a block down the street. The designations "veterans of World War II" and "nonveterans" were another widely used line of demarcation. In many churches, age, marital status, and gender were the lines of demarcation used to distinguish one adult Sunday school class from another.

The ecumenical movement of the 1960s introduced a new slogan. "Instead of focusing on what separates us, let's lift up what we have in common."

As long as that was simply a wish or a slogan, no one was concerned. The reason it is placed first in this list of points of discontinuity is because (a) many churchgoers, especially those born after 1945, began not only to believe but also to make decisions on the assumption that this was valid and useful advice; (b) the people who preferred to focus on the differences that separate one religious tradition from another began to disappear; and (c) few church leaders of the 1950s would have believed the drive for ecumenism could produce the results it has this quickly.

Among the many consequences are (1) the continued increase in the number of interfaith and interdenominational marriages; (2) an unprecedented migration of second, third, fourth, and fifth generations of American-born Roman Catholics into Protestant congregations; (3) that remarkable coalition of Catholics, Protestants, and Jews organized against racial segregation in the 1960s; (4) a huge variety of Catholic-Protestant cooperative ministries on the local level; (5) the emergence of congregations replacing denominational systems as the basic building blocks in ecumenism; (6) the unprecedented number of adults who now find it easy to shop across denominational boundaries as they search for a new church home; (7) that migration of younger adults from denominationally affiliated congregations to the nondenominational megachurches; (8) the decision by many candidates for the ordained ministry to choose a seminary on the basis of geographical proximity or a distinctive belief system rather than denominational affiliation; (9) the recent increase in the number of congregations concurrently affiliated with two different denominations; (10) the increase in the number of pastors concurrently serving two or three congregations from different denominational heritages; (11) the flood of denominational mergers in the 1960–90 era; (12) the continued life of the Consultation on Church Union first announced in 1962; (13) the growing number of Protestant and Catholic clergy sharing the clerical role in wedding ceremonies; (14) the move toward open communion and the recognition of one another's orders by the Evangelical Lutheran Church in America, the United Church of Christ, the Presbyterian Church (U.S.A.), and the Reformed Church in America and the probable next step of the adoption of the Episcopal-

ELCA Concordat; (15) the emergence of lay-oriented and ecumenical parachurch ministries such as Promise Keepers and Bible Study Fellowship; (16) the rapid recent growth of nondenominational publishing houses; (17) the huge audiences created by several television preachers; (18) the ongoing conversations between Roman Catholic and various Protestant leaders on "what we have in common" and how to prepare for eventual reunion; and (19) perhaps most significant in doctrinal terms, a gradual and continuing broadening definition of the answer to that age-old question, "What is the road to salvation?"[2]

That last item introduces what at least a few will argue is the most significant consequence of ecumenism. A substantial proportion of Christians were attracted to this religion, not because of a thirst for knowledge, but because of a hunger for certainty. John 14:6 is a current example of that hunger.

By its very nature ecumenism creates pressures to search for a common theological ground, for accommodation, for compromise, for tolerance, and for an affirmation of diversity. Thus ecumenism is widely perceived to be compatible with ambiguity.

In the contemporary American culture, many of the adults on a self-identified personal spiritual pilgrimage are looking for certainty, not ambiguity, on such doctrinal questions as Christology; baptism; church membership; Holy Communion; adultery; salvation; the ultimate source of authority; the birth, life, ministry, death, and resurrection of Jesus; and the central reason for the existence of worshiping communities.

This distinction between certainty and ambiguity frequently is articulated by astronomers, physicists, engineers, chemists, physicians, and other scientists who are active leaders in congregations that teach and preach certainty, not ambiguity. Thus one consequence of contemporary ecumenism has been to sharpen the distinction between those two institutional expressions of the Christian faith.

What does your congregation emphasize? Certainty or ambiguity?

Thus one consequence of the remarkable success of the ecumenical movement is that for many church shoppers the difference between ambiguity and certainty has moved far ahead of denominational affiliation as the most meaningful line of demarcation to distinguish one congregation from another as they look for a new church home.

Do you agree that the growth of ecumenism is the number one surprise on the ecclesiastical scene over the past four decades? Do you view it as a cause for alarm? Or as a sign of hope? That depends on your values, goals, and criteria for evaluation. Dozens of Lutherans, for example, who have invested decades of their lives promoting Lutheran unity view the first ninety-five years of the twentieth century as positive and the last five years as a disaster. By contrast, those who in 1959 saw the eventual reunion with Rome as a thousand years away now view it as a possibility for the twenty-first century. (Orthodox Christians are an exception to that generalization.)

Those who viewed the emergence of powerful denominational systems in the 1830–1960 era as an unnecessary evil may evaluate the current ecumenical wave as the number one sign of hope. By contrast, those pastors who are counting the migration of their members to other denominations and to independent churches may be less supportive. Those who are driven by the admonition that all must be one (John 17:20-26) may regard the contemporary ecumenical movement as the most hopeful sign in contemporary Christendom.

The Erosion of the Western European Religious Heritage

From this observer's perspective, and as one whose ancestors came to the United States from Bohemia and Germany, the second biggest surprise consists of three strands. One strand is the decreasing importance of European ancestry among third, fourth, fifth, and sixth generations of American-born residents whose ancestors were born in western Europe. These Americans tend to identify themselves by many other characteristics (age, gender, place of birth, marital status, education, occupation, political philosophy, place of residence, religious belief system, income, number of children at home, hobbies, and so on) rather than by ancestry. This trend is now a significant factor in strategy development among Mennonites, Baptists, Lutherans, the Church of the Brethren, and Roman Catholics. As recently as the 1960s, ancestry was a major factor in the self-identification of specific congregations. The adult children and grandchildren of those congregational leaders usually place a low value on ancestry as a source of either personal or congregational identity.

A second strand is the emergence and appeal to younger generations of American-born residents of what can be described as the "Made in America" religious traditions in general and American evangelicalism in particular.[3]

The third strand consists of those religious traditions in the United States that are organized around a western European religious heritage.

A persuasive argument can be made that the religious traditions in America that trace their origins back to western Europe peaked in terms of internal cohesion, numbers, capability to reach and assimilate newcomers, energy, creativity, vitality, enthusiasm for missions, a sense of institutional unity, and financial resources sometime during the 1950s and early 1960s. Their subsequent decline can be measured by the decrease in Sunday school attendance, the drop in the number of baptisms, the increase in the number and divisiveness of internal quarrels, the decrease in the number of new missions launched annually, the shrinkage in membership, their withdrawal from the large northern central cities, the rise in the annual death rate per one thousand members, the squeeze on the national denominational budgets, the decrease in the number of new members received each year, the reduction in the size of the national staff, the emphasis on institutional survival, and the move from resourcing to regulating congregations.

The other side of that picture is represented by the increased number of congregations that either do not carry a denominational label or are affiliated with a Made in America tradition. Examples include the Christian and Missionary Alliance, the Seventh-Day Adventists, the Churches of Christ, the Wesleyan Church, the Church of the Nazarene, the International Church of the Foursquare Gospel, the Church of Jesus Christ of Latter-day Saints, The Church of God in Christ, the Calvary Church Movement, the Vineyard Movement, The Church of God (Cleveland, Tenn.), the Assemblies of God, and at least a hundred Holiness denominations. Next door to them are the fully "Americanized" religious traditions that carry their European heritage very lightly. Examples include the Southern Baptist Convention, the Evangelical Free Church of America, the Conservative Baptist Association of America, and the Evangelical Covenant Church.

A third category includes several Christian bodies that can claim American origins but now closely resemble the western European religious heritage. The most highly visible example is the United Methodist Church. The Methodist Episcopal Church of 1784 has been described as the first holiness denomination in American history, and it clearly was a Made in America religious tradition at that time.[4] Several of what are strong contemporary holiness religious bodies, such as the Wesleyan Church and the Church of the Nazarene, trace their origins back to Methodist holiness preachers.

Over the past dozen decades, however, the combination of (1) ever-closer relationships between Methodist officials and leaders from western European religious traditions, (2) the move to place polity ahead of doctrine in the belief system, (3) the replacement of sanctification of the individual with preservation of the real estate and sending money to headquarters as the number one responsibility of the congregation, (4) ecumenism, and (5) the requirement that candidates for ordination graduate from a western European type of theological school have moved this denomination into the regulatory role of the western European religious traditions.

In a similar manner the influence of their theological schools, mergers, and the ecumenical movement have moved the Christian Church (Disciples of Christ) and the United Church of Christ to a point where they have more in common with the European Reformed traditions than with the Made in America religious movements.

Perhaps the most widely discussed consequence of this gap between the western European religious heritage and the Made in America institutional expressions of Christianity came in the late 1990s.

On one side were the supporters of and participants in the movement called Promise Keepers. They came largely from (a) those in the Made in America religious traditions, including the independent churches and movements such as the Vineyard; (b) ministers and laymen in congregations that are affiliated with a denomination with a western European heritage but that carry that affiliation very lightly; (c) leaders in the various renewal movements in those western European traditions; and (d) those who emphasize a close personal relationship with the second person of the Trinity.

The critics came largely from those adults with close ties to a western European religious heritage who placed a high value on (1) the authority of the confessions, (2) a high view of the authority of the institutional expression of the church, and (3) the importance of the first person of the Trinity. Many of them also brought serious doubts about the validity of any Spirit-led religious movement, while others protested the absence of women.

In somewhat overly simplistic terms, the gap was between those who are comfortable with an institutionally generated agenda and those who are comfortable with a Spirit-led movement.

One inconsistency in this analysis is that at least a few of the leaders in the Made in America branch of Christianity, who otherwise were supporters of the Promise Keepers movement, articulated reservations when the movement began to attract a growing number of Roman Catholics. These same leaders, however, are completely open to "cradle Catholics" joining one of their congregations.

While several exceptions exist, a useful generalization comes in response to the question, What are the numerically growing religious bodies in the United States? A simple answer is the Made in America religious traditions, including that growing number of independent churches, are experiencing numerical growth. The greater the influence of that western European religious heritage, the more likely that religious body is shrinking in numbers as the annual death rate among the members climbs. The notable exception to that generalization is the Episcopal Church, which benefits from the upward mobility tendencies of ecclesiastical migrants.

Among the many differences between the Made in America religious traditions and those that represent a western European heritage are these: (1) the western European heritage tends to emphasize the transcendence of God the Creator, while the American evangelical religious culture emphasizes a personal relationship with Jesus the Savior; (2) the European tradition tends to design worship to strengthen the faith of believers, while the American tradition assumes worship also can persuade the nonbeliever of the truth and relevance of the Christian faith; (3) the congregations in the American tradition tend to project higher expectations of believers than do the congregations in the western European tradition; (4) the European tradition is more supportive of a legalistic approach to church polity, while the American polity assumes that a congregation—and especially a denominational relationship—reflects the nature of a voluntary association (some European traditions even go so far as to refer to the "courts" of the church and channels for appeal); (5) in the European tradition the pastor's ministry is supposed to be evaluated by peers, while the American tradition affirms the fact that the crucial evaluation will be by the parishioners; (6) denominational and local traditions are far more influential in planning and decision making in the western European heritage, while evangelism and a future-oriented view are more powerful in the Made in America churches; (7) the Made in America churches are more comfortable with a consumer orientation, while the western European heritage churches are dominated by a producer stance; (8) congregations in the western European tradition tend to focus on assimilating new members after they have joined, while the American style is more likely to expect newcomers will be assimilated before they formally unite with that church; (9) the western European churches tend to see "joining this church" as a destination, while the American approach tends to conceptualize membership as a doorway that should lead to discipleship; (10) overlapping those two characteristics, most congregations in the European tradition are somewhere between surprised and delighted when the ratio of average worship attendance to confirmed membership exceeds 80 percent, while many American-style churches assume that ratio will and should be far above 100 percent; (11) one explanation of those contrasting ratios is that the European tradition makes it easy to become a member and difficult to become an ex-member, while the Made in America approach usually has a high threshold at the entrance into membership and a low threshold at the exit; (12) the European tradition is more attractive to the person who is comfortable with the social worker approach to ministry (help the hurting, feed the hungry, shelter the homeless, counsel the troubled), while the American religious culture often is more attractive to the person who is a self-identified evangelist; (13) leaders in the Made in America churches tend to be more comfortable with the emergence of the megachurch than are their counterparts in the western European tradition; (14) the western European tradition values the acoustic sound in music, while the American churches are more accepting of the electronic sound; (15) the institutional expression of the western European religious heritage is organized around distrust of congregational leadership, while the Made in America religious bodies usually display a high level of trust in congregational leaders; (16) the western European traditions usually place a high value on the confessions, the teachings that emerged from the Reformation, and the traditions of that religious heritage, while the Made in America religious bodies are more likely to focus on Scripture as the sole source of authority; (17) the western European heritage congregation often will seek a pastor or senior minister who will lead that congregation in attaining its goals, while the Made in America churches tend to be more open to the pastor who challenges the people to fulfill the potential God has placed in that congregation; (18) over the years the western European liberal tradition has grown increasingly comfortable with ambiguity on doctrinal issues, while the American style tends to teach and preach certainty; (19) the western European tradition often defines a parish in geographical terms, while the American tradition is more likely to define a congregation by what it does in ministry and/or by what it teaches; (20) the corporate worship of God in the western European tradition tends to place a high value on an intellectual approach to the faith, while the Made in America traditions usually place a greater emphasis on an experiential approach to the faith; (21) in recent decades the Made in America religious bodies have been far more effective in exporting their religion to other continents than have their western European counterparts; and (22) the western European heritage tends to conceptualize community ministries (a child-care center, the feeding of the hungry, the sheltering of the homeless, a recreation program, and so forth) as community service projects. By contrast, the Made in America culture is more likely to conceptualize these as components of a larger evangelistic strategy. (American Unitarianism is one big exception to this distinction.)

Do you view the numerical growth of the Made in America religious traditions as a source of hope or as a cause for alarm?

The Fourth Great Awakening

In September 1995 the recent Nobel Prize winner in economics, University of Chicago professor Robert W. Fogel, gave the Bradley Lecture. In this lecture he declared the United States was currently in its fourth great religious revival. He went on to add that the current religious reawakening "is fueled by a revulsion with the corruptions of contemporary society." Fogel dated the beginnings of this Fourth Great Awakening to about 1960. He emphasized that one expression of this current religious revival can be measured in the sharp increase in the number of adherents to what he defined as "enthusiastic religions."

While some of us may disagree with 1960 as the beginning date for this contemporary religious revival, a growing number of people agree it is a reality. Did it begin in 1976 with the election of Jimmy Carter to the presidency? Or in 1985? Or in the 1960s with the emergence of the interfaith coalitions in the Civil Rights movement? The historians of 2075 will be able to speak to that question with greater confidence than we can today.

The signs of this Fourth Great Awakening are all around us today. Those signs include the rapid numerical growth in the churches that exalt the second and third persons of the Trinity; the huge increase in the number of adults engaged in serious and in-depth weekly Bible study groups (the number meeting at the place of work is estimated to have doubled between 1988 and 1998); the arrival of a new era in Christian music; the many books with a spiritual theme on the bestseller lists; the rapid growth in the number of Christian day schools in religious bodies in which that is not a part of their tradition; the rapid growth in the number of congregations with a full-time or part-time minister of prayer; the shift in emphasis in theologically conservative congregations from law to grace; the creation of thousands of new worship experiences designed as "seeker-sensitive services"; the recent growth in the number of white upper-class and upper-middle-class suburban house churches; the attraction of over two million adult males to the Promise Keepers movement and the creation of more than twenty thousand men's Bible study and prayer groups that have emerged from that movement; the numerical growth in the membership of non-Christian religious bodies in the United States; the election of two Southern Baptists to the presidency and vice-presidency in 1992 and their easy re-election in 1996; the increasing number of large metropolitan daily newspapers that have replaced the weekly religion page with a four- to eight-page religion section; the rapid growth in the number of Protestant laity entering a full-time Christian vocation; the emergence of the Charismatic Renewal Movement back in the 1960s (which represents one good reason to date the beginning as about 1960); that remarkable growth in recent years in the number of seminary-trained pastoral counselors in private practice; the emergence of several "networks" that link quasi-independent and independent congregations together in a nondenominational movement; the huge increase in the number of weekend spiritual retreats designed for the laity; the number of persons who enroll in a theological school as a means of enriching their personal spiritual journey but who display no interest in ministry as a paid vocation; the increasing number of popular network television programs with a spiritual or religious theme; the increasing sensitivity of elected political leaders to the "religious vote"; the recent rapid growth in the number of congregations launching off-campus ministries designed to reach people in the "pre-Christian stage of their faith journey"; the growth of American evangelicalism while many of the churches carrying a strong western European religious heritage are experiencing numerical decline; the recent increase in the number of adults choosing a religious vocation as their second (or third or fourth or fifth) career; the growth in the number of high school students engaged in regular in-depth Bible study; the increase in the time allotted to a period of intercessory prayer in the typical Sunday morning worship service from a couple of minutes to a quarter to one-half hour; the emergence of the spiritual growth movement; the requirement in many theological schools that incoming students complete at least one course in spiritual formation; the classes for believers designed to help them improve their skills in articulating and sharing their faith; and the shift in many congregations from the former priority given to converting nonbelievers into believers to the current top priority of helping believers become fully devoted followers of Jesus Christ (a growing number of congregations have raised transforming believers into disciples as the top priority at the old campus and have launched several new off-campus ministries where the top priority is persuading inquirers, skeptics, doubters, searchers, seekers, pilgrims, agnostics, and self-identified disillusioned ex-church members of the truth and relevance of the Christian gospel).

Those represent a few of the signs that Professor Fogel was right. The United States is involved in a new religious revival!

Before reflecting on the consequences of the arrival of the Fourth Great Awakening, seven other trends and patterns of ecclesiastical behavior should be added to the mix. Together they help to explain the great discontinuity of the 1990s with the 1950s. The first is the gradual erosion of that western European religious heritage discussed earlier. The second is the recent rapid growth of the American evangelical religious culture. The third can be seen most clearly in retrospect. It began in the 1960s. Before then, it was widely assumed that younger people should be socialized into the culture by older people. The children born in the 1920s were socialized into the American culture by their parents, by other respected older adults, by the Great Depression of the 1930s, and by World War II.

A new pattern emerged with the babies born in the late 1940s and the 1950s. Partly because of their numbers, but largely because of changes in our society, these young people were greatly influenced by their peers in the 1960s and 1970s. Most of them threw away the rule book prepared for them by their parents and other older adults. They wrote their own rule book. The most highly visible example of this was a rebellion against the traditional dress codes. In the 1950s women wore gloves to church. Today gloves are worn by dentists at work. A second, which is discussed in chapter three, is the demand to be entertained.

Far more significant than the rebellion against the old dress code, however, was the rebellion in music. Jim Muertha, who had made his living promoting classical music, recalled, "Basically, we've lost two generations of listeners.... What happened was that in the sixties, you lost the generation that didn't want to listen to anything that parents liked. So they went off into rock music—the hippie generation. And then when they had kids, they really couldn't pass along a love or interest in classical music because they didn't know anything about it."[5]

Perhaps the most highly visible place to encounter the new contemporary Christian music is in those congregations—and most of these were founded since 1990—that are composed largely of adults born after 1968 or 1969. Many of them focus on one slice of the new music, and each congregation can be recognized by its "signature" music that speaks clearly to one segment of these young adults.

As interest in classical music waned, record companies cut back on classical recordings to less than 4 percent of the market; radio stations stopped broadcasting classical music; young people did not choose to learn to play the organ; newspapers stopped covering classical music concerts; the egalitarian movement declared all music to be equal; and rock, pop, country, and western music began to build huge followings.

As a result, a 1996 study by the National Endowment for the Arts reported that classical music performances drew most heavily from people born in the 1936–45 decade.

Among the victims was classical Christian music—a loss mourned largely by people born before 1947.

A fourth part of this context is that the babies born in the 1950s and early 1960s grew up with television that presented a faster pace of life in a world filled with color. Television did not teach children to love classical music. MTV and *Sesame Street* taught new generations that people should interact with what they see and hear and that effective communications include color, music, spoken words, motion, repetition, visual images, a change of pace, humor, drama, trust, surprises, and interaction.

Sitting and listening to a concert of classical music was a comparatively passive experience.

The fifth part of this discontinuity with the past overlaps what Dr. Fogel described as the "enthusiastic" religions. Younger generations seeking to discover meaning in life seek out congregations in which the people are enthusiastic about their faith as Christians, where they are comfortable talking with others about their personal relationship with Jesus, where the worship of God is a participatory experience, where it is acceptable for people to raise their hands in praise and thanksgiving during worship, and where the norm is not passivity but enthusiastic and active participation in all expressions of congregational life. Typically these congregations challenge people by projecting high expectations of anyone who seeks to become a full member; they display a low level of ambiguity about what they believe and teach; and they expect members to advance in their personal faith journey from passive believers to active disciples of Jesus Christ.

These high expectation and high commitment congregations are attracting a disproportionately large number of churchgoers born after 1955.

A sixth part of that discontinuity with the past has been largely overlooked. Up through the 1950s, most of what both congregations and denominational systems did had a unifying effect on the constituency. Examples include helping people survive the Great Depression of the 1930s, building and nurturing large adult Sunday school classes, raising money to support world missions, holding revivals, rallying people in support of the Allies in World War II, transmitting the faith to younger generations, supporting denominational colleges and other institutions, providing worship opportunities, planting new missions, arranging church picnics, constructing new church buildings to replace obsolete facilities, singing the hymns everyone knew and loved, coming to the aid of families in distress, and worrying about the threats posed by Roman Catholicism.

For the past four decades much of what congregations—and especially denominational agencies—have been doing has been perceived by many as highly divisive. Examples include a new era of Christian music; denominational debates on American foreign policy, the ordination of women, abortion, divorce, sex education, homosexuality, affirmative action; involvement in the Civil Rights movement; the collection and redistribution of monies by denominational headquarters; multiculturalism; new forms of worship; community outreach ministries; the racial integration of churches; new styles of preaching; the criteria used in the selection of delegates to denominational gatherings and in the filling of denominational staff vacancies; new attitudes toward baptism; the curriculum to be used in the Sunday school; involvement in world missions; confirmation classes for youth; biblical interpretation and theology; the planting of new missions; and the rise of the megachurches.

With one major exception, most of what American Christians engage in today can be described as divisive. Regular churchgoers choose up sides and quarrel over dozens of concerns and questions. The one major exception is prayer. As Stanley Perea has pointed out, unlike music, preaching, a philosophy of missions, biblical interpretation, and worship, prayer is the one thing in which Christians engage in a cross-cultural setting that is unifying.

Therefore, in what is an increasingly multicultural American culture, it should not be surprising that a renewed emphasis on the power of intercessory prayer is a central component of Promise Keepers and many other expressions of the Fourth Great Awakening.

Finally, a seventh part of the discontinuity created by the Fourth Great Awakening can be described as a normal, natural, and predictable response when change is viewed as threatening. That is denial. Denial is the natural response when a man is told he is terminally ill. Denial is a normal response when a husband, who has let work become his mistress, discovers his wife is leaving him. Denial is a predictable response to the process of growing old. The thirty-nine-year-old baseball player who is given his unconditional release after a season filled with disappointments tells reporters, "I believe I can play in the majors for another two or three years."

When leaders in the traditional Christian bodies in the United States are asked to reflect on the Fourth Great Awakening, a natural response is denial. Others dismiss it as a passing fad, often using language that resembles the words used by the Episcopalians and Congregationalists in the early years of the nineteenth century to minimize the significance of the rapid numerical growth of the Baptists and Methodists.

Unfortunately, denial never has been a source of creativity, innovation, or renewal.

When these seven overlapping changes are combined with the coming of the Fourth Great Awakening, it is not surprising that this belongs on the list of the great surprises of the last third of the twentieth century.

The most obvious consequence is that this Fourth Great Awakening has changed the mix of religious life in America. The congregations that identify with it are growing in numbers, while many of those that reject it are shrinking in size or closing.

A second consequence is an increasingly bitter debate over what is the "right" way to do church and what is the "wrong" or heretical way.

Overlapping that is the polarization of the leadership in several denominations. Those who identify with the forces fueling this contemporary religious revival usually are on one side of these intradenominational quarrels, while their opponents often represent a western European religious perspective.

While it is not a highly important issue, for some of us who are mature adults, one consequence is the need to learn a new system for classifying congregations. The old system that was widely used in the first several decades of the twentieth century declared that the five most useful lines of demarcation for classifying congregations were these:

1. Denominational affiliation.
2. Racial or nationality heritage of the members.
3. Place on a theological spectrum that stretched from fundamentalism on the right to Unitarianism on the left with conservative, evangelical, neo-orthodox, and liberal scattered between the two extremes.
4. Location of the meeting place—rural, small town, suburban, or central city.
5. Size as measured by membership or average Sunday school attendance.

Today the most useful lines of demarcation for classifying congregations into smaller groups have been altered by the Fourth Great Awakening. From this observer's perspective, the twenty-seven most useful lines are these:

1. What is the ethnic composition of the membership?
2. Is worship focused primarily on the first or the second or the third person of the Holy Trinity?
3. Does this congregation convey a sense of ambiguity or an expression of certainty as it proclaims the gospel?
4. Is the primary focus in the allocation of scarce resources (staff time and energy, money, space, volunteers, and the like) on (a) taking care of the members or (b) reaching nonbelievers with the good news of Jesus Christ?
5. Does this congregation hold all weekend worship services in the same building? Or two different sites? Or five? Or ten? Or fifty? Or one hundred?
6. Does this congregation project high expectations of anyone seeking to become and/or to continue as a member? Or low expectations? (In some congregations the require-

ment for being continued on the membership roster is (a) the contribution of money at least once a year and/or (b) attending worship at least once every year.)

7. Does this congregation represent a western European religious heritage or a Made in America evangelical Christian stance or neither?

8. What is the size of the congregation as measured by the average worship attendance on the typical weekend?

9. Has that number been going up or down during the past ten years?

10. What is the median tenure of today's members?

11. Is the median age of the baptized membership rising or dropping?

12. Are decisions driven primarily by local and denominational traditions or by a clearly defined mission statement and ministry plan?

13. Does this congregation operate a Christian day school as one component of a larger package of ministries with families that include children?

14. Has this congregation been worshiping in the same room since before 1970?

15. How many different opportunities are offered every weekend for the corporate worship of God? One? Two? Three? Four? Five?

16. Is corporate worship designed on a presentation model or a participation model?

17. Is program planning driven by a producer or a consumer orientation?

18. What proportion of the regular attendees reside at least five miles from the meeting place?

19. Was most of the music used in worship created before 1960? Or in 1960 and later?

20. Does the finance committee have direct access to bequests and to the income from trusts or from an endowment fund?

21. Is the number one priority in the assignment of volunteers maintaining the institution (acting as trustees, teaching, serving on the finance committee, singing in the choir, serving on boards and committees, and so forth) or identifying, enlisting, training, placing, and supporting volunteers in off-campus ministries?

22. Is the congregation served by a full-time, paid minister?

23. If served by a full-time resident pastor, did the current pastor arrive during the past eighteen months?

24. Where is the meeting place located? (Rural, small town, central city, or suburban?)

25. Where is this congregation on a theological spectrum that runs from fundamentalist to extremely liberal?

26. What is the income level of the regular attendees in worship?

27. What is the denominational affiliation of the congregation?

In other words, it is easy to identify two dozen lines of demarcation that are more meaningful than the denominational affiliation in classifying congregations.

A far more significant consequence of the Fourth Great Awakening can be described by four migrations.

The largest is the migration of millions of adults out of the religious tradition in which they were reared into a congregation that represents several facets of the Fourth Great Awakening. At least seven or eight million of these migrants are adults who were reared in the Roman Catholic Church and at least that many more were reared in a Protestant congregation that represented a western European heritage.

The second migration is from denominationally affiliated congregations into independent or nondenominational congregations.

A third, and smaller, migration consists of (a) Protestants into Roman Catholic parishes and (b) adults moving from a congregation that focuses primarily on the second or third person of the Trinity in worship to one that exalts the first person of the Trinity.

The fourth, and smallest, of these four migrations consists of American-born blacks and the American-born children and grandchildren of immigrants from Asia, Africa, Mexico, and Central and South America into predominantly Anglo congregations. By 2030 this could be the largest of these four migration patterns.

For many leaders, both congregational and denominational, the number one issue can be stated in a few words. Do you believe a great religious revival is underway in the United States? Those who do will plan from a different set of assumptions than those who deny it.

Finally, while of minor importance, one of the consequences of the Fourth Great Awakening in hundreds of communities is the existence of two ministerial associations. One is for ministers from congregations and religious institutions identified with a western European religious heritage, and one is for pastors from congregations in the American evangelical stream.

Do you view the Fourth Great Awakening as a sign of hope? Or as a source of alarm? Or do you deny it is happening?

From Cooperation to Competition

From a personal perspective, one of the greatest surprises of the past four decades, and by far the biggest disappointment, is now widely, if not universally, accepted. This also is a source of concern and disillusionment among many pastors who were socialized into the parish ministry in the 1960s and 1970s, when intercongregational cooperation was in the same pantheon of values as God, motherhood, and apple pie. Many of them regard the word "competition" when used to describe the relationship between two congregations as absolute proof the devil is still alive and at work in the world.

Intercongregational cooperation in member-oriented ministries and programs (worship, teaching, evangelism, spiritual formation, etc.) is not compatible with numerical growth. After many years of encouraging intercongregational cooperation, this was a hard lesson for me and many others of my generation to accept.[6]

Intercongregational cooperation in community witnessing, striving for social action, speaking with a prophetic voice on issue-centered ministries, planting new missions, camping, offering degree-level seminary classes, working to alleviate world hunger, resettling refugees, coming to the aid of victims of a natural disaster, or ministering to individuals in jail or prison can be a productive strategy.

On the other hand, the joint operation of a Christian day school or the cooperative vacation Bible school or the union Thanksgiving or Good Friday service or the cooperative youth program involving two or three congregations or the joint Saturday evening worship service or the cooperative weekday child-care center or the joint confirmation class tend to (a) be organized around the lowest common denominator in terms of a belief system, (b) gradually become perceived as community-service programs rather than avowedly Christian ministries, (c) blur the distinctive identity of each participating congregation, (d) tempt the staff and the leaders of the continuing ministries (child-care center or school or youth program) to conceptualize this as a separate empire rather than as an integral part of the larger ministry of that congregation, and (e) reduce the attractiveness of what otherwise could be a significant entry point for newcomers into the life and fellowship of a particular congregation.

The obvious consequence is the question, How do the leaders of congregation A view congregation B that meets in a building across the street or down the road? As an ally? As a partner in ministry? As a comrade in a common cause? Or as a competitor in reaching newcomers to this community who are looking for a new church home?

Overlapping that is the future of the local ministerial association. Who belongs? Who are the dependable leaders in it? Back when intercongregational cooperation was the theme, it was relatively easy to build and maintain a broad-based and inclusive ministerial association. For a variety of reasons many communities now are served by five ministerial associations: (1) the one that includes clergy, both Roman Catholic and Protestant, serving churches with a western European heritage; (2) the predominantly Anglo evangelical ministerial association: (3) the African American ministerial fellowship; (4) the Korean or Asian group; and (5) the one composed of program staff members in the very large churches.

Experience suggests the number one reason for two or more congregations to bring together their ministries in worship, in teaching, in evangelism, in spiritual formation, and/or in working with youth or retirees is that this can be an effective prelude to designing a strategy to merge those congregations into one worshiping community.

From Doctrine to Polity

One of the central themes of American Christianity for most of the twentieth century was the quest for Lutheran unity. While the various strands of Lutheranism in America differed substantially in polity and language, they shared a common western European heritage. Most also shared a common confessional and doctrinal stance. One result was a series of denominational mergers. A total of seven major denominational mergers in the 1917–88 period that involved a combined total of twenty different Lutheran bodies reduced the number of Lutheran denominations in the United States from twenty-four in 1906 to approximately twenty in 1998. Most of the discussions leading to the various mergers focused on finding a common ground in doctrine.

Many ministers in the United Methodist Church accept the tremendous differences in the belief systems of the clergy in that denomination. The range is from one inch to the right of Unitarianism at one end of that spectrum to fundamentalism at the other end.

Given those huge differences in doctrine, plus other differences on such divisive issues as abortion, financial subsidies, homosexuality, the role of women, and multiculturalism, why has that denomination not divided into several more homogeneous denominations? While divided on doctrine, it is held together by polity.

In recent years, ecumenism has moved doctrine to a secondary position in the efforts to increase interdenominational cooperation. One example of that was the 1957 merger that created the United Church of Christ. Despite substantial differences in both doctrine and polity, that merger was consummated. A second example is in the Presbyterian Church (U.S.A.) polity which has moved ahead of doctrine as the litmus test in evaluating candidates for ordination.[7]

The most notable example of the higher priority placed on polity came in the summer of 1997 when the Evangelical Lutheran Church in America narrowly rejected the proposed Concordat with the Episcopal Church because of differences in the role of the episcopacy but easily approved the Formula of Agreement with three denominations in the Reformed tradition, despite vast differences in doctrine. That approval also may have terminated the quest for Lutheran unity that had been going on in the United States for two centuries.

For this observer to see Lutherans place polity ahead of

doctrine in ecumenical discussions constitutes one of the great surprises of the past four decades.

One of the consequences is the increase in the number of students who choose a theological school on the basis of its doctrinal stance or geographical proximity or reputation rather than on denominational affiliation. If doctrine is a secondary issue, why spend more money to go to a denominational seminary?

A second consequence is the advantage gained in the competition for future new members by those congregations which stand for certainty, rather than for ambiguity, in their teaching and preaching.

A third consequence is a product of the fact that for many people doctrine is a more powerful force than polity in reinforcing a sense of identity and internal loyalty within a congregation. When doctrine ceases to be a cohesive force, what will replace it? Loyalty to that long-tenured pastor? Missions? The building? Friendship ties? The group life?

Fourth, the erosion of a distinctive denominational doctrinal stance has made it easier for unhappy church members to migrate to another congregation. The big winner in this has been and is the independent congregation with a clearly and precisely stated doctrinal position.

A fifth consequence is a product of the fact that the general pattern is for the very large congregations, regardless of denominational label, to be congregational in polity. In those religious traditions with a strong connectional polity, this can produce a feeling of alienation among the leaders in the smaller churches who feel they are being forced to "follow the party line" while the "tall steeple churches" go their own way.

Sixth, it no longer is safe to assume that the new minister will bring the same doctrinal stance as the predecessor simply because both were ordained in the same denominational tradition. This is but one of many factors behind the increasing number of "mismatches" between pastor and parish.

Seventh, as was mentioned earlier, polity has moved ahead of doctrine as a major barrier to proposals for increased cooperation among denominations or for a new round of denominational mergers.

Finally, from a pastoral perspective, it no longer is safe to assume that every adult coming in by an intradenominational letter of transfer adheres to the same belief system being taught and preached in this congregation.

From Low to High Expectations

For generations it was widely assumed that (1) each new generation would be theologically more liberal than their parents' generation; (2) congregations—and denominational systems—naturally would drift toward the left of the theological spectrum, and this was a natural, normal, and predictable consequence of the upward mobility of the constituency and of the trend toward more formal education for the clergy; (3) one consequence of those two trends was that the frequency of worship attendance by the members gradually would decline as the decades rolled past; (4) new religious movements from the theological right would emerge to serve the lower classes, and these new religious bodies would project high expectations of their constituents in terms of behavior, moral values, orthodoxy, and religious commitment; and (5) the long-established religious bodies would continue to serve the well-to-do, the better educated, and the upwardly mobile. One observation used to describe this trend said that the children of the new converts in the fundamentalist church would become members of the Church of the Nazarene. Their children would become Methodists. The children of the Methodists would join the Presbyterian Church, and their children would switch to an Episcopal parish. Social mobility and religious mobility moved together and in the same direction. That also was not an unrealistic description of contemporary trends in the first half of the twentieth century. Straight-line projections suggested these trends would continue through the rest of the twentieth century.

With three surprising exceptions, those trends have continued over the past half century. For many congregations that had been drifting toward the low expectation end of the spectrum for several decades, the big surprise came when the new pastor arrived and began to move that congregation in a reverse direction toward high expectations. Frequently this was accompanied by (1) an increase in the worship attendance, (2) the replacement of aging and long-tenured volunteer leaders by younger people, (3) a drop in the median age of the membership, and (4) the exodus of thirty or more longtime, but now unhappy, members who left in protest—and six months later were not missed.

A common pattern was for the recently arrived pastor to explain to a few wise, open-minded, deeply committed, and influential leaders, "This congregation was founded many decades ago as a high commitment covenant community. Gradually it has drifted in the direction of becoming a voluntary association that projects low expectations of those who want to become a member of this fellowship. It seems to me we have two choices. One is to relax and continue to drift into tomorrow as a church with low standards for becoming a member. A lot of people do prefer that type of church. The alternative is to reverse that pattern. The best way to do that, if you believe that is the direction the Lord wants us to go, is to gather a couple of dozen of our key leaders together in a weekly Bible study group. Together we can discern the New Testament model for a worshiping community. That would give us direction in our planning for a new day. What do you think we should do? Whom should we invite to join us in that Bible study?"

For many people a bigger surprise came when they saw the large numbers of well-educated and financially successful adults who were appearing as enthusiastic volunteer leaders in rapidly growing and relatively new congregations that usually are on the conservative half of the theological spectrum and are either (a) affiliated with a religious movement that came into existence after 1829 or (b) carry no denominational label. The highly visible examples include the Church of Jesus Christ of Latter-day Saints, the Seventh-Day Adventists, Islam, and a variety of congregations in which the average worship attendance exceeds the reported membership by a three- or four- or five-to-one ratio. The point of commonality is that they all project high expectations of anyone seeking to become a full member.

A third exception in that general drift toward low expectations can be seen in the growing number of youth groups in the churches and in parachurch organizations that project high expectations of high school students. These expectations often include daily Bible study, prayer, fasting, tithing, service, sacrifice, and commitment to the core values of that group.

To state it in historical terms, in scores of communities four of the five largest Protestant congregations in 1958 were churches that projected low- to mid-level expectations of anyone seeking to become a member. Forty years later, four of the five largest Protestant churches in those communities are high expectation and high commitment covenant communities.

That is a big surprise to those who assumed the drift toward lower and lower expectations was a permanent trend in American Christianity.

The most obvious consequence of this shift from low to high expectations is expressed in the plea of the pastor who asks, "How do I transform a low expectation church into a high commitment parish?"

A second is the statement of the minister or the denominational leader who responds to that question by declaring, "Life is too short to focus on renewing the old. I am going to devote my time, energy, gifts, and skills to organizing new missions that will be high commitment churches from day one."

A third is the mature parent who has been a lifelong member of low- to mid-level commitment congregations and now is perplexed, pleased, and curious to discover his or her children have left that tradition to join a high expectation church.

From this observer's perspective, this recent increase in the number of congregations that challenge people with high expectations ranks up there with the Fourth Great Awakening as two of the most hopeful signs of the times. A third sign of hope is the product of a long-term trend that began more than two hundred years ago.

The Ministry of the Laity Has Arrived

One of the distinctive differences between the European religious heritage and the American evangelical culture concerns the role of the laity. Most of the former display a basic distrust of the laity in general and local leadership in particular. The big exception to that generalization has been the various denominational organizations created, owned, and operated by and for women. Many of these, however, have had long-running battles with the central ecclesiastical bureaucracies.

By contrast, most of the Made in America religious traditions display a far higher level of trust in the laity to create, own, staff, and operate new ministries. A current example of this conflict over the role of the laity is in the varying responses to Promise Keepers.

Many readers will contend that this point of discontinuity with the past should be placed at the top of the list of signs of hope. The record is clear! When challenged, when offered the appropriate type of training experiences, when the ecclesiastical structure is encouraging and supportive, and when the assignment is ministry, not administration, the laity are responding in huge numbers and with extraordinary effectiveness.

The highly visible examples include the churches with several dozen off-campus ministries staffed by lay volunteers; the creation of thousands of new house churches; the volunteer teams that spend a few weeks to several months on mission-work trips; the new expressions of ministry being created, organized, and staffed by the laity such as Habitat for Humanity and Bible Study Fellowship; the caregivers trained in the Stephen Series; the growing network of prayer ministries; the unprecedented number of prison ministries; the thousands of smaller congregations staffed by a bivocational part-time lay minister or by a bivocational team of three to seven laypersons; the phenomenon referred to as contemporary Christian music; and the lay volunteer teachers of those weekly adult Bible study and/or prayer groups that meet in homes, offices, restaurants, hospitals, and dormitories.

Several observers of the contemporary religious scene contend the expanded role of the laity is a central component of the new definition of orthodoxy.

What are the forces behind this recent expansion in the ministry of the laity?

Number one, of course, is a larger institutional context organized on the assumption that the laity can be trusted. This contemporary expression of the ministry simply is not compatible with an ecclesiastical system built on distrust of local leadership.

Number two is a congregational context that projects high expectations of everyone seeking to become a member.

Number three is a recognition that many adults are on a self-identified religious pilgrimage. That pilgrimage begins with the seeker or searcher or skeptic or inquirer who eventually is persuaded of the truth and relevance of the Christian faith and becomes a believer. The believer is encouraged to become a learner, and learners are challenged to become disciples. Disciples are invited to identify both their gifts and their passions for ministry, and the relevant training experiences are designed and offered to equip these disciples for doing ministry.

Instead of organizing congregational life around the traditional subjects (worship, Christian education, fellowship, care of the real estate, and money raising), that congregation is organized to help pilgrims progress from seeker to believer to learner to disciple to apostle.

For those concerned about organizational systems, this also stands out as one of the biggest consequences of an affirmation of the ministry of the laity.

Number four on the list of forces behind this movement is the professionalization of a large segment of the population. Once upon a time, in terms of years of formal education, the pastor was the best-educated person in that congregation—and frequently one of the two or three best-educated persons in the whole community.

Today the pastor may rank no higher than one hundred and ninety-third among people in that congregation in terms of competence in financial administration; eighty-seventh in understanding the early intellectual, social, and emotional development of young children; seventeenth in counseling skills; two hundred and forty-fifth in managerial skills; twenty-fourth in the study of the Old Testament; seventy-ninth in working with teenagers; fifty-eighth in skill as a teacher; and ninety-second in competence in music skills.

The basic generalization is that the larger the congregation and/or the younger the constituency, the larger the number of the laity who will be more competent than the pastor in that area of ministry.

One consequence of that is a redefinition of the role of the paid staff from people who are paid to do ministry to trainers, challengers, scouts looking for gifted people to serve as colleagues on a ministry team or to serve as resources for volunteers doing ministry, or encouragers.

This has led to discarding the old planning model based on a scarcity of talent and replacing it with a planning model based on an abundance of gifted people.

Finally, a compelling force is the recognition that for most Christians it is a more rewarding and satisfying experience to be involved in doing ministry than in doing administration.

Among the many consequences are (1) the discovery that the ministry of the laity flourishes in high expectation churches, (2) a growing shortage of jobs for ordained male generalists trained to do ministry, and (3) the growing recognition that one of the responsibilities of a worshiping community is to transform the lives of people—and part of that process is to challenge and equip them to do what they know they cannot do.

Do you identify this as a sign of hope or as a threat to the vocational future of the clergy?

The Redefinition of Women's Ministries

Nearly all of the long-established denominationally created systems for women's ministry began with world missions as the central rallying point. Women who were deeply committed Christians came together to create single-gender support systems for world missions.[8] Their histories constitute one of the most inspiring success stories in American Christianity during the nineteenth and early twentieth centuries.

The operational assumption was that women who are deeply committed Christians could and should help in making foreign missions a high priority in their congregations. Those deeply committed women prayed for missions; they studied missions; they challenged young people to consider God's call to be missionaries; they raised money to fund missions; and they were influential and well-informed lobbyists for missions.

One of the most valuable bits of advice ever given to agents of planned change is, "You never can do only one thing!" Every victory in implementing new ideas inevitably produces unanticipated consequences.

A relevant example can be found in those congregations that are effective in persuading adult women who are nonbelievers of the truth and relevance of the Christian gospel. As these women reflect on the transformation the gospel has brought to their religious pilgrimage, they begin to ask questions. Many of these questions can be summarized under the broad umbrella of, "What else have I been missing? How else can this worshiping community nurture me in the faith? What must I do to move from the status of a believer to become a fully devoted follower of Christ?"

One result is the greater the effectiveness of a worshiping community in transforming agnostics, doubters, inquirers, searchers, seekers, skeptics, and other women on a self-identified religious quest into committed believers, the greater the demand for ministries that focus on the concerns these new believers bring to church.

The old approach to women's ministries focused on those who were deeply committed Christians and who also were determined supporters of world missions.

The new approach focuses on the personal and spiritual journeys of women of all ages and roles.

The old approach encouraged every congregation to include a women's organization that usually focused on missions, study, prayer, fellowship, and money-raising.

Frequently that larger organization met four to ten times a year in a general meeting and was divided into circles or study groups that met monthly. A common pattern was a morning circle, an afternoon circle, and an evening circle.

The new approach is based on the assumption that the needs of today's women vary greatly and no one program or organization can meet all these needs. This can be illustrated by the components of the women's ministries in one high expectation, eight-hundred-member congregation that includes about twelve hundred constituents.

Bible Study. Three different approaches are offered at three different times—Tuesday evenings, Wednesday mornings, and Thursday afternoons.

Heart to Heart. A one-to-one mentoring ministry that pairs women with common concerns, experiences, and dreams, often across generational lines.

Divorce Recovery Workshop. This is a Tuesday evening, two-hour time for women currently involved in the process of divorce.

Believercise. Two sets of classes, each meeting three times a week, for exercising to Christian music. A great chance to meet and make new friends!

New Mothers. This class is offered Monday evenings and Saturday mornings for expectant and new mothers. It focuses on how to appropriately stimulate and nurture the intellectual, emotional, and social development of babies.

Women in the Workplace. A support group meeting monthly for women employed outside the home.

Prayer. Four prayer cells meet weekly for one hour of intercessory prayer.

Women's Missionary Ministry. Monthly meetings are held and this is a support system for missionaries in the field and on furlough.

The Empty Nest Club. This is primarily a fellowship,

crafts, mutual support, and study group for homemakers who have watched their last child leave home.

Women in Community Ministry. This group enlists, trains, places, and supports women who serve as continuing volunteers in various community organizations, including an ecumenical adult day-care center, the local hospital, the food pantry, a shelter for the homeless, and similar expressions of ministry.

The Phoenix Circle. This is a mutual support group for women in their second or subsequent marriage.

Mothers of Preschoolers. This mutual support group meets twice a month and includes classes on parenting. A great place to meet and make new friends!

The Surrogate Grandmothers' Club. This group of grandmothers is the number one support system for the five-mornings-a-week nursery school for four-year-olds.

The Brides' Club. This group is for women who are about to marry and/or are newlyweds. It is a high energy, high turnover, and high expectation group of women who are about to enter a new stage of the life cycle.

WHO. This is a group of widows who help one another and help others deal with widowhood.

The Coed Volleyball League. This is a league of twelve coed teams who play volleyball from mid-November to mid-March. Each team plays twice a week.

The Vocationally Challenged. This is a weekly gathering with a fairly high turnover of women of all ages who feel God may be calling them to either a part-time or full-time Christian vocation.

In addition, that church offers overnight women's retreats in late April and in mid-October every year.

This expression of a contemporary women's ministry not only illustrates the discontinuity with the older model, it also illustrates (1) the range of needs and expectations people bring to church today, (2) the increased complexity of contemporary parish ministry, (3) the ways specialized ministries can be attractive entry points for newcomers, (4) the obsolescence of the one-size-fits-all approach to ministry, (5) the shift from a producer's agenda to a consumer-driven model, (6) possibilities in intergenerational programming, (7) the contemporary trend toward increasing the number and variety of choices offered people, (8) the shift from supporting denominational causes to responding to the needs of the constituency, and (9) perhaps most important, the possibilities to design ministries around both a person's faith journey and the life cycle.

From a larger perspective, the women's missionary organizations founded in the last half of the nineteenth century were created on a foundation of exclusion. Women were excluded from policy-making positions in both congregational and denominational structures. The women's missionary organizations opened one door for women to utilize their gifts as leaders, innovators, and visionaries. But that door opened to an agenda originally designed and articulated by men.

The new expressions of women's ministries are based on inclusion and designed to be responsive to the needs of today's women. This new agenda has originated with women! This is a 180-degree shift and may be the greatest event of discontinuity discussed in this book.

Among the consequences of this evolution in ministries with women, four stand out for this discussion. The most obvious is the difficulty 95 percent of all Protestant congregations encounter when they compete for future new members with churches like this one that can offer a broad array of attractive entry points for women. In the old model the congregation with three circles in the women's missionary organization could compete with the large church that had a similar organization only on a larger scale with ten circles.

Far more subtle is the way the old model reinforced (a) the

loyalty of the individual women to their denomination and (b) the relationships of each congregation to their denominational system. This new model provides many attractive entry points for newcomers. It also reinforces the individual's attachment to that congregation, but it does little to undergird denominational loyalty.

Third, the most widely ignored consequence can be summarized in one question. Who will transmit our denominational heritage and instill a strong denominational loyalty in future generations?

In the 1950s the answer was, "We will depend on our denominational seminaries to do that with the next generations of ministers; we will depend on parents to do that with their children; we will reinforce that with the materials we use in our Sunday school and confirmation classes plus our youth ministries with teenagers; we expect our summer church camps and our denominationally affiliated colleges to do that with our young people; we expect our regional judicatories will do that with our volunteer lay leaders; and perhaps the most influential of all, we know our women's missionary organization will do that with women and girls."

Most of the components of that system have been weakened in recent years. Candidates for the ministry go to regional seminaries or to university divinity schools; today's children are less likely to inherit institutional loyalties from their parents than was the pre-1960 pattern; parachurch organizations are supplying an increasing proportion of the teaching materials used by churches; volunteer lay leaders go to nondenominational retreat centers and to parachurch training events; and the women's organizations focus on older women or switch their focus to a customer agenda.

Fourth, instead of asking the pastor to come and return thanks to God before eating lunch at the monthly (or quarterly) general meeting, the new model places a heavier burden on the paid staff.

Highly competent staff is required to create, nurture, and coordinate this extensive ministry; to identify, enlist, train, place, and support the volunteer leaders who are essential to this model; to be sensitive to and to design new ministries in response to new needs; and to identify and respond effectively to potential problems before they grow into crisis proportions. Usually the large regional church finds it easier to staff this ministry than does the small neighborhood congregation.

From 30 Percent to 1 Percent

Back in the 1950s it was relatively easy to find a church in rural or small-town America in which one third or more of the local residents were constituents. That could be 30 percent of the several hundred residents living within three or four miles of the meeting place. The open country church might include more than one-half of the nearby households as members.

The combination of the erosion of inherited institutional loyalties, the widespread ownership of the private motor vehicle, good roads, the growth of individualism, the increased geographical separation of the place of work from the place of residence, and the growing competition for the loyalty of the consumer has transformed American society. One result of that is the replacement of the small neighborhood worshiping community by the large regional church.

One consequence is that most institutions have been narrowing the definition of their constituency. As recently as 1965 a two-block stretch of Main Street might have been lined with two grocery stores; a bank; a savings and loan office; the post office; two five-and-ten variety stores; two drug stores; a dentist's office; an office-supply store; a hardware store; two taverns; a cafe; a jewelry store; a meat market; a dry cleaning establishment; a new car dealership; two churches; two gasoline stations; a physician's office; an insurance office; a small department store; a funeral home; a hotel; a Sears, Roebuck store; a J. C. Penney store; a paint and wallpaper store; and an optometrist's office.

In the typical month, a resident living a few blocks away may have entered at least a dozen of those establishments. If that community included 5,000 residents within the corporate limits plus another 4,000 in the surrounding trade area, most of those entrepreneurs assumed they had at least 2,000 to 6,000 potential customers.

The larger of those two churches on Main Street reported nearly a thousand members, or more than 10 percent of the population of the trade area. With 400 baptized members, the smaller of the two could claim well over 4 percent of the area population as its constituents.

Thanks to the expansion of the urbanized area around a nearby city, that small community with 5,000 residents in 1965 has grown to a population of 19,000. The central business district of that nearby city lies sixteen miles to the east of Main Street.

Seventeen years ago that 400-member congregation on Main Street purchased a thirty-two-acre site six miles to the east and constructed new buildings, including a Christian day school that opened nine years ago. It draws people from a fifteen-mile radius, and the current population of that circle totals 275,000. With 2,700 baptized members, that congregation now serves 1 percent of the residents of its service area.

A mile to the south is the building that houses an independent congregation launched only twelve years ago. Thanks to the highway network, it also draws people from a fifteen-mile radius. During a typical month approximately 1,200 different people worship with that congregation. That is less than one-half of 1 percent of the population of the service area, but most observers believe that reaching an average worship attendance of 800 in only twelve years is a remarkable accomplishment.

Back in 1965 that 400-member church on Main Street had a slogan on the bulletin board facing the sidewalk. It read, "Everyone welcome." Today its primary appeal is to parents who (1) own at least one motor vehicle, (2) desire a high-quality education based on a traditional Christian value system and traditional standards of ethical behavior for their children, (3) are comfortable in a congregation composed largely of adults born after 1950 who reflect an upper-middle-class lifestyle, (4) express strong upwardly mobile ambitions for their children, and (5) prefer a traditional Eucharist-centered liturgical service for the corporate worship of God, including a large, robed choir, a pipe organ, and a presentation-type preaching.

A mile away that fast-growing independent congregation has designed its ministry to persuade casual self-identified Christians to become eager learners and to challenge those learners to become fully devoted followers of Jesus Christ. Their 1200 "adherents" include 300 deeply committed adult members—and that provides the necessary foundation of enthusiasm, money, volunteers, creativity, and energy. They expect that by their twentieth anniversary close to one-third of 1 percent of the 275,000 residents of their service area will have climbed that high threshold to full membership—but they also assume that by the end of twenty years, approximately one-half of the 900 adults who have joined will have moved away.

"If we have 400 resident adult members eight years from now who are fully devoted followers of Jesus Christ, I won't complain," explained one member in affirming the fact that high commitment churches often experience high turnover in the membership.

What had been the larger of those two congregations with meeting places on Main Street still worships there. While the population of the city has nearly quadrupled, their average worship attendance has dropped from 700 to slightly over 400.

The most significant consequence of this overall trend can be condensed into one word. FOCUS.

The most obvious example of this can be seen in the obsolescence of a favorite model for new church development of the 1865–1950 era. This called for planting a new mission to reach and serve the families moving into those new residential subdivisions. This model was still widely used in the 1950s, the 1960s, and the 1970s. It was widely assumed that a new mission could and would reach 10 percent of the projected 5,000 residents of these new homes. A few that were launched by the high-energy mission developer with a magnetic personality exceeded that goal. Many, many more reached 1 or 2 or 3 percent of the population. Together they produced the term "arrested development" to describe the new mission that plateaued in size with an average worship attendance of 35 to 85.

The replacement model in new church development calls for reaching one-half of 1 percent to perhaps as many as 2 percent of the 100,000 to 400,000 residents who live within ten to twenty miles of the meeting place of that new mission. That is achieved by focusing on a precisely and narrowly defined potential future constituency.

A second and far more common example is the shrinking and aging congregation founded before 1960 that is now served by a sixty-year-old pastor who is counting the days until retirement. Many of the members also are counting because they are confident that if the successor is a thirty-five-year-old, handsome, extroverted, attractive, articulate, deeply committed, gifted, personable, and high-energy father with a beautiful wife and two adorable children, a flood of young families will fill the pews and classrooms. They completely overlook the fact that there is a severe national shortage of committed churchgoers born in the 1960s and 1970s who are eager to rescue dying congregations. (That raises another question. Why are the theological schools failing to produce scores of graduates who are both called and competent to resurrect dying churches?)

The basic generalization is the larger the size of the congregation and/or the longer it has been in existence and/or the greater the degree of obsolescence in its real estate and/or the larger the population of that community and/or the higher the turnover rate in its ministerial leadership and/or the faster the growth rate of the area population and/or the larger the number of new missions founded since 1980 and/or the older the members of that congregation, the more likely that congregation has two choices. The easy one is to grow older and smaller and eventually merge with one or more other congregations. The more difficult is to focus its resources on identifying and responding to the religious and personal needs of a narrowly, precisely, and clearly defined slice of the population. In urban and suburban America, it is rare today to find a Protestant congregation that is able to reach and effectively serve 5 or 10 or 20 or 30 percent of the residents of its service area.

That is one more reason why it is more difficult to be an effective parish pastor today than it was forty years ago.

From Lover to Leader

The eighty-three-year-old retired minister was being honored by friends and relatives on the sixtieth anniversary of his ordination. A fifty-five-year-old guest asked, "As you reflect on your years as a very successful pastor, what advice do you have for the young people of today who are going into the parish ministry?"

The instant reply was, "Preach the Bible and love the people! That's what I've been advising young pastors for the past forty years."

That was excellent advice for most pastors for most of the past three or four centuries on the North American continent. It affirmed the merits of good biblical preaching and of the pastor's role as a shepherd. It continues to be good advice for at least one-half of the bivocational ministers serving small congregations. It also is relevant advice for denominational leaders and seminary professors to offer if the goal is to increase the number of congregations averaging fewer than 85 at worship.

The changes of the past three or four decades that are discussed in this book suggest that that advice should be heard as an incomplete sentence.

Better advice for pastors serving congregations that (1) average more than 120 at worship or (2) have agreed their distinctive call is to persuade nonbelievers of the truth and relevance of the Christian faith or (3) are focusing on transforming believers into disciples or (4) are concentrating on reaching the generations born after 1955 or (5) are full-service churches averaging more than 1200 at worship or (6) now are large regional congregations or (7) have chosen to be Kingdom-building churches is to recognize that that simple bit of advice is inadequate for today's challenges.

Today's version of that advice should be expanded into a seven-part sentence. Preach the Bible, love the people, earn their trust, challenge them to do what they know they cannot do, equip them to meet those challenges, support them in their ministries, and be prepared to respond creatively to the future consequences of present actions.

The precise wording of that sentence is open to negotiation, but it is offered here for four reasons.

1. To illustrate a central theme of this book. It is far more

difficult and challenging to be an effective pastor today than it was in the 1950s.

2. The expectations projected of an effective pastor are far greater than they were in the 1950s.

3. The day of the ministry of the laity has arrived!

4. While all of the world still loves a lover, what most congregations will need for an effective ministry in the twenty-first century is challenging and effective leadership.

This growing recognition of the value of competent leadership is both a threat to many and a sign of hope to others.

The New Sources of Resources

While it is not the most important change to occur on the ecclesiastical scene, a persuasive argument can be that the greatest point of discontinuity with the past is in where congregations turn for help.

Back in the 1950s, most congregations depended on their denominational system for Sunday school materials; for counsel in a capital funds campaign; for hymnals; for expertise in education, worship, evangelism, and stewardship; for guidance on the appropriate organizational structure; and for such events as summer church camps, revivals, conferences, and workshops. With the exception of the Episcopal Church, only a tiny number of congregations depended on the denomination for financial assistance.

Ministers looked to the denominational system for their seminary training, for ordination, for accountability, for mutual support, for help in finding a position as a parish pastor, for an occasional continuing-education experience, for inspiration and affirmation, for news of denominational activities that was not carried on the grapevine, for a dependable pension system, and for their institutional identity.

Congregations and pastors both looked to the denomination to create and operate ministries that were beyond the capability of any one congregation. That included enlisting, training, placing, and supporting missionaries in other parts of the world; planting new missions; creating and administering a variety of institutions such as homes, camps, and schools; pioneering new forms of ministries; speaking the prophetic word in the public square; operating a publishing house; and participating in ecumenical discussions.

During the past four decades, three trends have transformed that scenario. The first is the increasing complexity of parish ministry has encouraged many more congregations to seek help. Second, for a variety of reasons, most denominations have not been able to expand their capability to resource congregations. Third, the combination of greater complexity and stiffer competition for future new members has made obsolete the old approach that one program or one conference or one strategy or one approach to ministry will fit all sizes and shapes of congregations.

The demand today is for customized resources designed for a specific constituency or for one particular congregation or one need.

The result of these changes and demands is a proliferation of resources available to congregations seeking help. Instead of looking solely to their national denominational headquarters and/or their regional judicatory, congregations have access to scores of places to turn to in their quest for help. That marketplace has expanded at least twentyfold in four decades.

The marketplace includes a growing number of parachurch organizations, independent publishing houses, theological seminaries, profit-making corporations in music, independent parish consultants, church-related colleges, independent entrepreneurs, private fund-raisers, architects, management consultants, authors, retreat centers, and state university programs of continuing education for the clergy.

The newest kid on the block is the self-identified teaching church. This is the congregation that has enjoyed a remarkable track record in several phases of the parish ministry and has been persuaded it should share what it has learned with others. These congregations, and today their number exceeds three hundred, have earned a high level of credibility by their performance. The typical format is to offer a two-to five-day workshop led largely by paid staff and volunteers from that teaching church. The participants come to see, experience, and hear described an effective model of contemporary ministry, to be introduced to new ideas, to be able to question those who are doing it, and to discern the difference between a philosophy of ministry and a ministry plan. They are encouraged to come as teams of five to twenty leaders and to go back home to adapt (not adopt) what they have learned to their unique situation. This teaching church may turn out to be the most effective way to resource congregations in the twenty-first century. In a few cases this will turn out to be a three-party partnership including one or more teaching churches, a publishing house, and a theological school with classes held on the campus of every teaching church in that partnership.

The most obvious consequence is whether denominational leaders perceive these partnerships to be a gift from God or the creation of the devil.

One of the consequences of this trend is a weakening of the power of a denomination to transmit to future generations the culture, values, teachings, traditions, heritages, and distinctive identity of that particular Christian tradition.

For some, the most threatening consequence will be the need for denominational systems to define their reason for being. Others will describe that as an overdue and welcome challenge.

For a few of us, the emergence of these teaching churches, each with a constituency that includes participants from a score or more of denominations plus others from independent congregations, simply verifies the contention that resources for congregations should be tailored to local needs rather than to fit a particular denominational tradition or dream.

Others point to the crowds of participants at the events offered by the teaching churches as the number one evidence of the success of the ecumenical movement.

The Endangered Species List

For many, the biggest surprise to come out of the past four or five decades is the identity of those religious institutions with a questionable future. In the 1950s it was widely assumed that the congregations most vulnerable to the changes in American society were (1) the small rural church, (2) the small inner-city congregation, and (3) the Anglo church meeting in a building located in a racially changing neighborhood.

The trends of the 1990s suggest that the congregations near the top of the endangered ecclesiastical species list are the churches averaging 85 to 200 at worship. They are too large to offer the attractive assets that are found in the best of the small congregations and too small to be able to compete in quality, choices, and opportunities with the large regional churches. (A growing number of pastors argue that suburban congregations need to average at least 500 to 700 at worship to be able to mobilize the resources required to compete with those regional megachurches.)

This represents tremendous discontinuity from that day when an average worship attendance of 300 or more generated the response, "That is a BIG church!"

Those who bring a broader perspective to this question may argue that on the list of endangered religious species, the congregations averaging 85 to 200 may rank no higher than seventh.

The number one endangered species may be the large university founded by Protestant Christians and designed to transmit the Protestant Christian faith to future generations. In addition, it was assumed that that college or university also would transmit the values, traditions, and dreams of that particular religious body to future generations and thus create new generations of advocates and apologists for that branch of the Christian faith. This effort has produced scores of what today are first-class, private, nonsectarian, and well-endowed universities. Some are neutral about Christianity. In others, many of the faculty are somewhere between critical of and hostile toward Christianity.

Number two on that list of endangered religious institutions may be the American Catholic universities. In 1990 the Vatican decreed that the bishops of the church should exert more authority over the Catholicity of the universities within their jurisdiction. That document, "Ex Corde Ecclesiae," was issued to reverse the trend toward the secularization of Catholic universities in America. It has run into the American demand for academic freedom. Which will prevail? Don't bet against academic freedom in the United States!

Perhaps number three on that list are the thousands of Protestant congregations that have enjoyed a comfortable era ministering with several generations of American-born residents from a western European ancestry who grew into adulthood in the 1920–60 era. As those generations of churchgoers gradually disappear, these congregations reach a fork in the road. The attractive path is labeled, "Keep on doing ministry as you have always done ministry. The road that brought you to this point will take you far into the twenty-first century." The other path warns, "Change! Adapt to a new era! The road that brought you to this point leads into oblivion!"

The history of American Christianity suggests a majority of these congregations will choose the first road and only a minority will make the changes required to reach and serve new constituencies born after World War II and/or those who do not trace their ancestry back to western Europe.

Clearly among the top four on this list are the Roman Catholic parishes being closed because of the shortage of celibate, male priests. Some will survive with a nun as the resident pastor, but many more will close.

Today's world includes large numbers of ministers who would prefer to focus on two responsibilities, preaching and shepherding. Likewise at least ten million Protestant church members want a pastor who will excel in two phases of ministry, (1) preaching the Bible and (2) loving the people. Unfortunately most of those ten million Christians are scattered among the 180,000 Protestant congregations that can neither economically nor vocationally justify having their own full-time and fully credentialed resident pastor. Most have been priced out of the ministerial marketplace.

As a result, the supply of ministers who would be delighted with the dual role of preacher and lover exceeds the market demand.

At the other end of the size spectrum are the 35,000 Protestant congregations who not only want a pastor who is a far above average preacher, who excels in interpersonal relationships, and who is a deeply committed Christian, they also need a minister who is an entrepreneurial and visionary leader, who can earn the trust and confidence of the members, who can inspire people to do what they know they cannot do, who can lead a congregation as it seeks to discover and respond to God's call in ministry and mission, who can rally the people to fulfill the potential the Lord has placed in that church, and who can lead in creating the staff-volunteer teams required to carry out their ministry.

This is where the demand exceeds the supply. Too many people want lovers when the churches need leaders. At least a few readers will insist the number one problem is the over-supply of ministers who are neither lovers nor leaders.

Unless they are able to re-earn a reputation for their capability to resource congregations effectively, hundreds of denominational boards, departments, commissions, and agencies will disappear. Some will survive on a fee-for-service financial basis, but most will encounter serious problems. Whether the most casualties will be among the regional judicatories or in the national denominational headquarters remains to be determined, but the high-risk agencies tend to be in the national organizations.

At least a hundred residentially based theological schools, some are Roman Catholic but most are Protestant, occupy the sixth slot on this list of endangered ecclesiastical species.

Why is that list so long?

That requires an examination of a couple of dozen points of discontinuity in the secular context for ministry and of the consequences of those changes.

2
THE BIG SEVEN

If we shift the focus from the ecclesiastical scene to look at the most influential points of discontinuity in the secular world, seven stand out. Five of the seven represent policies and actions by the civil governments of the United States. A simple example is home ownership. Protestant congregations in the United States always have been more effective in reaching and serving homeowners than in reaching renters.

In 1900, 63 percent of all nonfarm dwelling units in the United States were occupied by renters. As recently as the 1920s there were three roads to home ownership: (1) inherit it; (2) save and pay the full price at time of purchase; or (3) take out a five-year loan at the bank and renew it every five years. When the Great Depression hit in 1929–32, many banks could not or would not renew that loan, and the borrower lost title to the house.

In the 1930s the federal government decided to encourage home ownership by guaranteeing payments on thirty-year mortgages. The proportion of nonfarm homes occupied by renters dropped to 59 percent in 1940, to 39 percent in 1960, and to 33 percent in 1997.

For several decades the federal income tax law has been designed to reward homeowners, especially those with high incomes and big mortgages, and to penalize renters.

One recent consequence of that policy of encouraging

long-term mortgages for homeowners is an increasing number of pastors who have purchased their own home rather than live in church-owned housing.

Now that banks and other lending institutions are accustomed to long-term mortgages, it is easier for congregations to negotiate ten- or twenty- or thirty-year mortgages.

From Deflation to Inflation

Far more significant, however, has been another point of discontinuity in the policies of the United States government. For most of American economic and political history, a period of inflation, often the product of a war, was followed by a deflationary period. As the accompanying table explains, at the end of the Civil War, the consumer price index was nearly twice the level of 1710 or 1833, but by 1898 it had dropped back to the level of 1710 or 1833 or 1860.

Inflation was followed by deflation. The deflationary period following the Civil War was followed by four years of inflation from 1897 through 1900. A brief two-year deflationary period was followed by eighteen years of inflation from 1903 through 1920. A five-year deflationary era followed, and then came the big inflationary wave of 1926–29. That brought the Great Depression and a seven-year deflationary period from 1929 through 1935. World War II brought a fifteen-year inflationary era. As of this writing, the consumer price index last dropped in 1955. Thus 1997 was the forty-second consecutive year in the longest inflationary period in American history.

The very old church members of today still recall, "We started to build a new church in 1929, but then the depression hit and we met in the basement until after the war. It was 1946 before we could build on top of that old basement."

Another old-timer declares, "You were lucky! We completed construction of our new church in 1930, and we lost it to the bank two years later when we couldn't make our payments."

CONSUMER PRICE INDEX

1710	=	25	1946	=	58
1814	=	53	1951	=	77
1833	=	25	1967	=	100
1860	=	25	1979	=	214
1865	=	49	1982	=	289
1898	=	25	1990	=	391
1914	=	30	1994	=	444
1920	=	62	1998	=	489
1933	=	39			

That generation was taught not to build until the congregation had enough money to complete the project.

One consequence of the current inflationary wave is that the building committee of 1967 learned the economic value of a long-term mortgage with a big balloon payment. They negotiated a $500,000 twenty-five-year mortgage with a $50,000 final payment in far-off 1992. Those who were still around in 1992 rejoiced in making that final payment with what they described as "twenty-five-cent dollars."

That generation was taught that the ideal church-building program should be financed by the largest mortgage possible payable over the longest possible period of time. Inflation is a friend of borrowers and an enemy of lenders.

Another consequence of the current forty-plus-year inflationary wave is due to the fact that in recent years the official consumer price index actually overstated the true increase in the cost of living. One result is the typical compensation package for a pastor (including salary, pension, housing, health insurance, and all other benefits) has increased at a more rapid pace than the increase in the total income of the congregation. Thus many congregations that could afford a full-time and fully credentialed resident pastor in 1955 have been priced out of the ministerial marketplace.

Add in the variable that more than one-half of today's Protestant congregations that were in existence in 1955 have shrunk in size in terms of average worship attendance. The consequence of those three variables (inflation, the overstatement of the rate of cost-of-living increase in the consumer price index, and the shrinkage in the size of many congregations) is that many denominations now have (1) an excess of fully credentialed clergy, (2) few or no attractive openings for new seminary graduates, and (3) a growing shortage of congregations that can both economically afford and institutionally challenge a full-time and fully credentialed minister.

A substantial proportion of the congregations that are being priced out of the ministerial marketplace are the neighborhood churches that averaged one hundred to two hundred at worship in the 1950s and now average sixty to a hundred at worship.

From Neighborhood to Region

Far less visible than the impact of inflation on the churches but far more influential in changing the secular context for ministry were two other decisions made by the United States government in the mid-1950s. Together these two policy decisions transformed the American marketplace, undermined the traditionally close relationships between place of work and place of residence, expanded the possibilities for people searching for a sense of community, and radically altered the context for church planning for the next several decades.

Together these two decisions accelerated the pace of a

process that was launched with the widespread ownership of the private automobile in the 1920s. That process has transformed the United States from a nation of neighborhoods into a nation of small regions.

The first, and the least widely discussed of these two actions, was the revision to the Internal Revenue Code enacted by Congress and signed into law by President Dwight D. Eisenhower in 1954.

The original intent of the legislation was to encourage the construction of new manufacturing plants and the replacement of obsolete machinery as a means of stimulating the economy. One economic motivation for achieving that goal was accelerated depreciation schedules for newly constructed buildings designed for income-producing purposes. The old tax legislation required forty years for the owner to recover the full costs of depreciation in calculating income taxes. The 1954 legislation made it possible to fully depreciate *new* construction in seven to ten years.

One result was to motivate investors to construct new buildings on the edges of the central cities or out in the suburbs, rather than to renovate old structures in the central business district. The large regional shopping center became a highly attractive tax shelter. Since it takes about two years for planning, land acquisition, and construction between the adoption of a new tax code and the resulting construction, the impact was not felt until 1956. In the seven-year period of 1949–55 inclusive, a total of 21 large regional shopping centers were opened in the United States. The seven-year period of 1956–62 saw an additional 199 open![1]

The old pattern saw suburbanites and residents of the central city going downtown to shop. That was where the big department stores were located.

The new pattern saw central city residents driving out to these new and attractive regional centers to shop.

History teaches that there is a normal lag of two or three

or four decades between the introduction of a culture-changing concept and the time when the churches begin to adapt to a new way of life. The old pattern of human behavior in North America recognized that people living outside the central business district would travel downtown to shop, but people living downtown would not drive ten or twenty miles out to the suburbs to shop. The old pattern also recognized that suburbanites would travel into the central city to worship, but central city residents would not commute out to the suburbs to go to church.

The revision of the Internal Revenue Code in 1954 and the emergence of the large regional shopping centers in the post-1955 era changed the first of those two traditional patterns of human behavior.

Three or four decades later, however, new generations of residents of the central cities were finding it easy to commute out to the regional megachurch that served a constituency living within a thirty-five-mile radius.

The change in the Internal Revenue Code that rewarded new construction not only encouraged the construction of hundreds of new retail shopping centers, it also undermined the economic vitality of the downtown department store, the neighborhood pharmacy, the one-screen motion-picture theater, the neighborhood hardware store, the family doctor with a solo practice, and the neighborhood grocery store. The changes in human behavior patterns initiated by the 1954 changes in the federal income tax law also helped to create a supportive social environment twenty years later for the emergence of the regional megachurch.

The second of these two changes that originated in the mid-1950s is the one President Dwight D. Eisenhower later concluded was the number one domestic accomplishment of his eight years as president and his favorite domestic program.[2] In February 1955 President Eisenhower sent a special message to Congress asking for a ten-year National

Highway Program. Five months later the appropriate legislation was approved in the Senate, but a coalition of Democrats, the CIO, and the railroads killed it in the House. The President wanted this new network of limited-access highways to go around the large cities, but in order to get the necessary votes in the House, the final legislation permitted construction in and through cities. In 1956 legislation was adopted that authorized the construction of 41,000 miles of the interstate highway system.

These two pieces of legislation led to the replacement of the neighborhood with the region as the basic unit in church planning.

Among the most highly visible consequences on the ecclesiastical landscape of those two national policy decisions made during the Eisenhower era are (1) the decision by hundreds of Anglo central-city congregations to relocate their meeting place; (2) the exodus of the predominantly Anglo mainline denominations from the large northern central cities; (3) the sharp numerical decline of thousands of Anglo congregations that chose to remain in the central city; (4) the sharp drop in the Roman Catholic population in many large central cities; (5) the emergence of thousands of new black, Latino, and immigrant congregations in the large central cities; (6) the growing number of congregations that have leased or purchased that thirty-year-old shopping center after the commercial tenants moved out and it became available as a low-cost meeting place; and (7) the emergence of the new regional megachurch as the successor to the old neighborhood parish.

Less widely discussed is another consequence. A "rural megachurch" once was an oxymoron. Today that is a viable option for those rural, small-town, and suburban congregations willing to redefine their service area as including a twenty- to forty-mile radius and able to implement a relevant ministry with thousands of urbanites who are comfortable with a ten- to forty-minute drive each way to church two or three or four times a week.

These two policy decisions from the mid-1950s have helped to make possible a new generation of megachurches in counties adjacent to the county that includes the central city of that metropolitan region. Most of these new regional megachurches are predominantly white, but a rapidly growing number are composed largely of immigrants from Asia or American born blacks or Latinos, and a few are genuine multicultural fellowships.

Many of the worshipers reside in the central city and commute to church via one of the segments of the interstate highway system.

These two policy decisions helped to pave the way for the marketplace to replace the neighborhood as people searched for a place to find community. These two policy decisions also helped to expand the range and variety of choices available to many Americans looking for a new church home.

From Community to Marketplace

Up until recently the Japanese culture was organized to reinforce a sense of community. One expression of this was the tradition of buying from local shopkeepers. The trade-off was reinforcing community cohesion at the cost of higher prices. Another expression of this was that most car owners built a relationship with the proprietor of the local gasoline station who also would make the necessary repairs when needed. The car owner knew that friendly relationships would reduce the chances of paying for unneeded repairs.

This was consistent with the larger Japanese economy, where jobs were for life and prices were controlled. It was a secure and comfortable world.

That economic order in Japan has been upset as younger

generations place a lower value on long-term relationships and shop for low prices.

The old emphasis on community is being replaced by the competition of the marketplace.

Older readers may interrupt by recalling, "That's the world in which I grew up! We shopped at the general store in town, and when my parents were short of cash, the storekeeper was always willing to extend credit. We never questioned the diagnosis of the mechanic at the local gas station when he described the repairs that were needed on the family car. I attended a four-year high school where every teacher could call every student correctly by name since there were only about one hundred and fifty kids in the whole school."

One of the most significant consequences of the emergence of the marketplace as the focal point for one's life is the change in building social networks. Once upon a time people socialized with their neighbors and their kinfolk. Frequently many of the neighbors were persons related by blood or marriage as well as by geographical proximity and by nationality, race, color, language, and citizenship. Farmers exchanged help with neighboring farmers. Homemakers found most of their friends from among the neighbors.

As the distant marketplace has replaced the neighborhood as a source of employment, as a place of entertainment, and as a place to purchase goods and services, the dynamics of building friendship circles have changed. Ask an adult to name his or her five closest personal friends. Frequently the list includes friends from the place of work, the place of worship, the regular gathering of a cohesive and homogeneous group, a service club or lodge or union, and similar circles, but not next-door neighbors.

In mid-1997 a survey of 1,009 adults conducted by the Scripps Howard News Service and Ohio University reported,

"The water cooler at work has surpassed the front porch, town hall and the local church as our major site of human contact." This survey reported that these adults experienced an average of thirteen significant face-to-face conversations every day. The men and women with full-time jobs reported that two-thirds of these significant discussions occurred at the place of work.

In commenting on this study, the syndicated columnist Bob Greene pointed out that this trend could be traced back to the 1970s to television's *The Mary Tyler Moore Show*. Before that, the television shows about people's daily lives had been based in the home. *The Mary Tyler Moore Show* pictured people in their place of work interacting with their coworkers.

If one looks at the ecclesiastical scene, this helps to explain the recent rapid increase in the number of large and growing regional churches. That is consistent with building one's friendship circle from among the people one meets in the marketplace.

The emergence of the marketplace as the successor to the neighborhood also helps to explain the increasing number of very small regional congregations as their members move to a new place of residence but are not replaced by newcomers to that neighborhood.

In mid-1997, when F. W. Woolworth closed the last of its variety stores, the columnist Bob Greene wrote a provocative essay. The theme of that essay can be found in two sentences, "But what people say they're going to miss comes down to that sense of finding everything in a small space. Of knowing there's a place full of friendly things, a place that is not outsized, that is not designed to overwhelm you."[3]

The giant shopping malls and the huge discount stores out on the edge of town have replaced the variety store on Main Street.

The Woolworth store on Main Street with its walk-in customers reinforced the sense of community. Those huge discount stores across the street from the twenty-year-old shopping mall represent the new marketplace. The generations born before 1935 grew up in a world that placed a premium on the sense of community. That was a culture that valued familiarity, continuity with the past, kinship ties, small institutions, simplicity, predictability, longtime relationships, informality, and a slower pace of life.

The generations born after 1955 have grown up in a culture that is organized around choices, competition, quality, large-scale institutions, rapid change, innovations, convenient parking, surprises, a nongeographical basis for creating social networks, anonymity, complexity, discontinuity with the past, and the drive of the new consumerism.

Bob Greene was right. People say they will miss the opportunity to shop in a small place full of friendly things. Bob Greene also was right when he pointed out in that same column that too few people were shopping there to keep these Woolworth stores open. The competitive marketplace had prevailed over nostalgia for the past. One of the beneficiaries of this trend has been that huge new discount store with the spacious parking lot. Another has been the new regional megachurch.

From Small to Large Scale

What do these have in common?
Professional football players? Milk containers? Dump trucks? Traffic lanes? Hardware stores? Elementary schools? Television screens? New car dealers? Teenagers? Airport terminals? Coffee cups? Bath towels? Corridors? Zoos? Feet? Closets? Paper clips? Libraries? Driveways? Cows? Elevators? Variety stores? Stomachs? Tractors? Bookstores? Banks? Lawnmowers? Houses? Hospitals? Gasoline stations? Airplanes? Motor vehicles? Grocery stores? Adults?

Bathrooms? Parking lots? Guns? Motion-picture theaters? Foundations? Neckties? Garages? Universities? Medical clinics? Dairy farms? Sites for new churches? T-shirts? Ice-cream cones? Telephone directories?

The answer, of course, is each one is larger than it was many years ago.

Protestant congregations should be added to that list. In 1890, according to the Census of Religious Bodies conducted by the United States Bureau of the Census, the 196,000 Protestant congregations reported a combined total of 14 million members who were invited to participate in the Lord's Supper. Those numbers produced a (mean) average of 71 members per congregation. By 1906 the mean for all Protestant congregations was 104 communicants per congregation. Exclusive of an estimated 50,000 small house-churches scattered across the country (which are not counted in the typical census of churches), the 1997 mean was at least 300 communicants per congregation and may have been closer to 350. That average in 1997 was 360 full members for the Church of God in Christ, 350 for the Evangelical Lutheran Church in America, 315 for the Lutheran Church-Missouri Synod, 390 (baptized members) for the Southern Baptist Convention, 235 for the United Methodist Church, 240 for the United Church of Christ, and 235 for the Presbyterian Church (U.S.A.).

One part of the explanation for the increase in the size of American teenagers is better diet. One part of the explanation for the increase in the size of the average Protestant congregation is urbanization. Another is increased competition. A third is the impact of government.

For sixty years state governments have devised financial incentives to facilitate the merger of public school districts. The United States Department of Agriculture has strongly and consistently encouraged the consolidation of farms. The policies of state and federal highway departments have encouraged the emergence of large regional retail stores. The policies of the federal government have encouraged the consolidation of hospitals and the creation of large medical clinics. The tax policies of the federal government have made it financially attractive for banks to merge. The differences in fuel consumption requirements set by the federal government have made it economically feasible for automobile manufacturers to produce and sell the highly profitable and large vans and utility vehicles. The research grants provided by the federal government have encouraged the creation of huge research-driven universities. The decision by the federal and state governments to subsidize the wear and tear on the highways has encouraged trucking companies to purchase huge trucks. The desire by cities to achieve a "world-class" status with a major league sports team and the willingness to subsidize that goal with public funds has produced huge sports stadia.

This list of examples could go on for a couple of more pages, but the point is simply to suggest that the emergence of the megachurch is compatible with governmental policies to encourage big institutions in all aspects of American life.

From the Old South to the New

"Wherever I go, I hear all of this talk that every congregation should be a growing church, but how do you expect my parish to grow when every year six to ten of my pillars, my most dependable leaders, and our most generous contributors retire to the west coast of Florida?" complained a Lutheran pastor in Pennsylvania.

"I know exactly what you're talking about," agreed a pastor from Iowa. "Every year we lose about twelve to fifteen of our most faithful families. Half of them are couples who move to Arkansas or Arizona to retire. The other half are younger leaders with two or three academic degrees and a high level of managerial or professional or technical skill who are moving to the South. Four of the twenty members who were on our church council three years ago now live in Arizona, five are in Austin, Texas, and one is in Louisiana. If you want to see the impact of the brain drain on parish leadership, come and look at my church."

Two of the most influential decisions ever made in Washington, D.C. were (1) the creation of the Tennessee Valley Authority and (2) the construction of scores of military bases in the South. Add to those two decisions the attractive climate discovered by Yankee military personnel stationed in the South; the decreasing price of electricity; air-conditioning; entrepreneurial leadership; a strong work ethic; a variety of factors that have created huge numbers of comparatively healthy and financially comfortable retirees in the North who dislike cold winters; jet aircraft; the interstate highway system; southern hospitality; comparatively low-priced land; the emergence of global markets; and federal and state tax policies; and one result is the new South.

One consequence is the decision by what had been northern regional immigrant denominations to transform themselves into national Americanized denominations. A second consequence was the decision by Baptists and Methodists in the South to plant new missions that grew into megachurches while their northern counterparts were cutting back on new church development.

A third consequence was the growth of the Southern Baptist Convention, which in the 1950s was still a largely Anglo, southern, and rural denomination. That recent growth has provided the institutional strength required for it to move into the North as part of a larger strategy to become a North American, multicultural, urban, and very large denomination with several hundred very large regional congregations.

The new South, along with the Southwest and the West

Coast, emerged as the most supportive environment for the growth of the regional megachurch.

That trend was facilitated by two other points of discontinuity with the past that are being experienced all over the North American continent. Neither of the two, however, is such a clear product of governmental action as the first five points of discontinuity discussed here.

From Relationships to Competition

The second half of this story about the impact of the marketplace also is illustrated by the emergence of WalMart as the successor to Woolworth. That story can be summarized in one word. Competition. In small-town America, as well as in Japan, retail trade rested heavily on relationships. The merchants depended on those long-term relationships with their customers.

The churches also relied heavily on relationships for replacements for those members who moved away, died, or simply dropped out. Kinship ties, neighborhood cohesion, denominational loyalty, marriages, and births combined to produce a new generation of members.

The combination of the arrival of new generations of younger people, the growing influence of the marketplace, and the availability of the private motor vehicle have (a) redefined the foundation for building community, (b) increased the competition for future customers among both the retailers and the churches, and (c) changed the landscape. One example is that the new WalMart store out on the edge of town has replaced the Woolworth store on Main Street. A parallel change is the numerical decline of First Church on Main Street and the emergence of that new megachurch on its fifty- or hundred-acre site out on the edge of town.

One example of the change in the retail marketplace is in

the sale of groceries. In 1980 the 21,000 conventional self-service supermarkets, the first of which was born in August 1930, accounted for 8 percent of all types of retail grocery stores and 43 percent of all grocery store sales. Fourteen years later the number of conventional supermarkets had dropped to 12,000 and they represented only 5 percent of all retail grocery stores. Their sales represented less than 21 percent of all grocery store sales that year.

The big change in the retail grocery business, however, was the increase in the number of the huge superstore- and warehouse-type grocery stores. They increased in number from 5,300 in 1980 to 12,500 in 1994. Their share of grocery store sales nearly tripled from 19 percent in 1980 to 52 percent in 1994.

It also should be noted that the specialized food stores selling only one or two lines (bakeries, meat markets, and so on) increased in number from 73,300 in 1980 to 87,000 in 1984, but their share of sales decreased from 6.6 percent in 1980 to 5.2 percent over fourteen years.

Finally, the combined number of convenience stores and superettes dropped from 146,000 in 1980 to 137,000 in 1994, but their market share held steady at 22 percent.

In summary, over a fourteen-year period those huge super-warehouses and combination grocery and drug stores nearly tripled their share of the market in grocery sales. While they represent only one-twentieth of all food stores, they now account for over one-half of all sales. Near the other end of the size scale, the convenience stores and superettes that constitute 55 percent of all food stores account for 22 percent of all sales in both 1980 and 1994.[4]

At this point the impatient reader may ask, "What's this got to do with the church in the twenty-first century?"

The safe answer is, "Maybe nothing." It is interesting to note, however, that a parallel trend has been occurring in American Protestantism. Where do people go to church in

America today? Among Protestant churchgoers the largest 6 percent of the congregations now account for nearly one-third of the worshipers on the typical weekend, and the smallest 60 percent of the churches account for 22 percent, a remarkably close parallel to the small grocery stores. The other 46 or 47 percent of the worshipers can be found in the 34 percent of all Protestant congregations that can be described as middle-sized. The number of small Protestant congregations averaging fewer than eighty-five at worship continues to increase, but their proportion of all Protestant worshipers on the typical weekend continues to decrease. Both trends parallel the increase in the number of specialized food stores that are dividing up a shrinking share of the food market.

The second coincidence reflects (a) the number of mid-sized grocery stores (the conventional supermarket) decreased by nearly one-half and their combined market share dropped from 43 percent in 1980 to slightly over 20 percent in fourteen years and (b) the number of midsized Protestant congregations also has been shrinking, but at a slower pace.

The central point of this analogy, however, is the impact of increased competition. The competition among retailers of groceries is without precedent in American history. One result of that competition is that a relatively tiny proportion of retail establishments now account for the sale of one-half of all groceries. The midsized stores are being squeezed out of the marketplace by the forces of competition.

Likewise the competition among churches for future adherents is without precedent in American church history. The congregations most likely to earn a repeat visit from a first-time worshiper are those that welcome newcomers, have a strong resource base, and can offer meaningful and attractive choices to people on a self-identified religious pilgrimage. The marketplace produces winners and losers among grocery stores and also among the churches.[5] The typical week sees at least sixty Protestant congregations in the United States choose to dissolve, disband, or merge into another congregation. That is easier than becoming competitive.

Back in the 1950s, couples with young children picked the neighborhood in which they would like to live, looked for a house that was on the market, purchased a home, and subsequently enrolled their children in the elementary school in that neighborhood.

Today many families begin that search for a new place of residence by first evaluating the choices among elementary schools, both public and private, deciding on what promises to be the best school for their children, and subsequently looking for a place to live. The educational marketplace has replaced the neighborhood as parents decide on where they live.

The marketplace has replaced the neighborhood as the place to seek community. One example of that is the increasing proportion of Americans who build their primary social network from people they meet at work and/or in church or some other voluntary association and/or from people who share their vocation or hobby rather than from among their neighbors.[6]

The marketplace also has raised the level of competition among variety stores, grocery stores, educational institutions, hospitals, and churches. That is a part of the changing context for church planning for the new millennium.

From Producer to Consumer

For many decades pharmaceutical companies introduced their new prescription drugs by articles in medical journals and by sending representatives out to call on physicians. In 1991, however, approximately $70 million was spent advertising prescription drugs directly to potential patients. The new goal was to reach the consumer of the drug, the patient. The hope was that the patient would ask the producer of the prescription, the doctor, to prescribe that new drug. By 1998 the amount spent by drug companies on consumer-oriented advertising had climbed to well over $1 billion!

The marketplace is beginning to replace the doctor's office as the place to introduce new prescription drugs.

This is but one example of another change in the context for ministry. "The customer is king" is the slogan for this new era. Instead of focusing on the product or service offered for sale, this approach to marketing begins by identifying the needs and concerns of the potential consumer.

One result is a highly divisive ideological debate among the clergy. One side contends, "We have been given the gospel of Jesus Christ to proclaim. Our responsibility is to proclaim that gospel faithfully, obediently, and accurately."

The other side responds, "What is accomplished if no one listens and no one responds? Our first responsibility is to establish a relationship based on trust that will enable communication to take place. After we have earned their trust, people will listen as we tell them about Jesus. We have to begin to build that relationship by being sensitive and responsive to their needs."

Those who want to proof text the first of these two points of view can point to the many times Jesus addressed a crowd and began with his message. Those who want to proof text the second position can point to the many times that Jesus began a conversation with an individual by asking where that person hurt.

In operational terms, the producer point of view is illustrated by the advertisements on the religion page of the newspaper that include the name, address, and telephone number of a congregation; the weekend schedule; the pastor's name; perhaps a denominational affiliation; and occasionally a sermon title and/or a slogan.

That same page also may include an ad by a church that uses a consumer-oriented approach. It usually begins with a question in big bold type. "Need help raising your children?" "Where do you plan to go to church on Christmas Eve?" "Are you in the middle of a painful divorce experience?" "Are your children beginning to ask questions you're not prepared to answer?" The rest of that ad describes how this church is prepared to help as you seek a response to that question.

A second example is the difference between two preachers. One preaches from the lectionary. The other prepares sermons based on concerns that surface from conversations with parishioners.

A third example is the producer-oriented church that has followed the same Sunday morning schedule for forty years. It begins with Sunday school followed by worship or worship followed by Sunday school followed by a second worship service that is a carbon copy of the first. Across the street the consumer-driven church offers four *different* worship experiences every weekend.

An interesting bit of trivia is the increased space available to consumers and the decreased space assigned to producers. The parking space at the bank for employees is less conveniently located than the parking lot for customers. The aisles at the discount store have been widened and check-out stations have been added, while the manager's office is somewhere between small and tiny. The narthex in that new church building is huge, but the senior minister's study is half the size of the office in a church building constructed in 1979. The waiting room at the HMO clinic is huge, but the physicians' offices are small. In 1940 the space for faculty parking at the state university was modest, but five times the space available for student parking. Today that ratio is reversed. Once upon a time, convenient parking spaces near a door at the church were reserved for the minister and other staff members. Today the most conveniently located parking spaces are reserved for mothers with very young children and for the physically handicapped. The staff park where they can find a vacant and unreserved space.

While many exceptions exist, the broad generalization is that persons born before 1942 tend to be more comfortable with the producer-orientation than younger generations who have been reared in a consumer-driven culture.

Which will drive the planning in your congregation as you design ministries for the twenty-first century? An emphasis on what your church offers? Or on what people seek as they look for a church that speaks to their religious and personal needs? Do you perceive this increasing emphasis on the concerns people bring to the churches as a sign of hope? Or as simply another surrender to the secular forces of consumerism?

3
NEW GENERATIONS BRING A NEW CONTEXT

———————— ⭒ ————————

What is the greatest single point of discontinuity in America between mid-twentieth-century and contemporary culture? A persuasive argument can be made that the answer is that most of the leaders and policy makers of the 1950s are dead or in nursing homes. Their successors have decided to walk in their own shoes rather than follow in the footsteps of earlier generations. This can be seen in the United States military organizations, in government, in higher education, in the practice of medicine, in the business world—and in the churches.

The seven points of discontinuity described in the previous chapter are, to a substantial degree, the products of governmental initiatives and/or the marketplace. All seven have changed the context for ministry. The additional eighteen points of discontinuity discussed in this chapter are, to a substantial degree, the products of births and deaths. New generations bring new perspectives and new agendas.

Since race, class, gender, and television have become the windows through which many of today's issues are analyzed, it is not surprising that several on this list reflect those perspectives.

From Racial Integration to Ethnic Separation

In 1970, sixteen years after the United States Supreme Court decision in the Topeka, Kansas school-desegregation case, the public high school in Hernando, Mississippi was desegregated. Within a few years what had once been an all-white school was largely black.

By 1997, however, that high school, a short distance south of Memphis, (1) was operating with a dual system of paid staff, including a black principal and a white principal, and a dual set of student offices and (2) had an enrollment that was 70 percent white.

Forty years ago eleven o'clock Sunday morning was referred to as the most segregated hour of the week. Today the most segregated hour of the week is lunchtime in many high school and university cafeterias.

One of the most remarkable developments of the 1960s was the creation of interfaith coalitions of Protestants, Roman Catholics, and Jews in opposition to racial segregation. For more than a hundred years Protestants had identified Roman Catholicism as a common enemy, and that was a unifying organizing principle among Baptists, Methodists, Presbyterians, and many others. Likewise, many Catholics identified Jews as an enemy.

That slice of American history was one reason these new interfaith coalitions struck many as a remarkable achievement. Racial segregation had joined Communism and anti-Catholicism as a major postwar common enemy and a powerful rallying point.[1]

Politically, American-born blacks began to become an influential factor within the Democratic Party in the 1930s. Thirty years later, organized labor (which for decades had barred blacks from the building trades), Jews, blacks, and the Civil Rights movement were united in building four decades of control of the House of Representatives.

Well before the end of the century, however, the forces favoring ethnic separation were beginning to change the culture. Monocultural ethnic minority caucuses were being organized within the Democratic Party, various denominational systems, organized labor, the United States Congress, and many high schools, colleges, and universities.

David Shipler has pointed out that this clustering into homogeneous subgroups has been and is a normal and predictable practice for centuries for people of all races, nationalities, religions, occupations, and social classes.[2] The greater the degree of heterogeneity in the larger group, the more likely that individuals will seek to be part of a relatively homogeneous subgroup that serves as a comfortable stability zone. In the churches, these often are called adult Sunday school classes, prayer groups, circles in the women's organization, caucuses, ministerial associations, choirs, singles groups, or Bible study classes.

A very large-scale example of clustering came in October 1995, with the Million Man March on Washington led by Minister Louis Farrakhan. It also represented the first officially approved and racially segregated march on Washington since a Ku Klux Klan demonstration in 1925. The Promise Keepers rallies of the 1990s were examples of interracial clustering.

By contrast, the 1960s brought an unprecedented degree of support for racial integration in American society. That created a new and, for many churchgoers, a highly stress-producing context for doing ministry.[3]

The 1990s, however, brought the continuation of a growing emphasis on ethnic separation. This time the leaders were not persons with a European ancestry, but members of ethnic minority groups. Examples of that include the designation of dormitories for specific groups on college and university campuses, the competition for funding and influence among various monocultural denominational caucuses, the growth in membership of monocultural professional organizations, the creation of nongeographical monocultural regional judicatories in various denominations, the quarrels between Korean shopkeepers and black customers in many large cities, and the organization of at least thirty new mono-cultural Protestant congregations for every one new multi-cultural mission.

An influential symbol of the move toward ethnic self-identification and ethnic separation can be seen in the categories used by the United States Bureau of the Census. The decennial census of 1950 used two categories (white and nonwhite). Three (white, Negro, and other) were used in 1960. That number climbed to seven (white, Negro, Indian, Japanese, Chinese, Filipino, and other) in 1970, and to nine in 1990. The Census of Population in 2000 recognizes these definitions of self-identification for Americans: Black, African American, Haitian, Negro, Hispanic, Latino, White, Alaska Native, American Indian, Native Hawaiian, Asian, and other Pacific Islander. Among the rejected categories were Arab, Cape Verdean, Middle Eastern, and Native American.

The parallel trend in the churches has been the vocabulary new generations bring to the self-identification of congregations—from Colored to Negro to Black to African American to Afrocentric, plus Caribbean-born, African-born, and racially integrated.

The complexity of this issue is illustrated by the 3 percent of the Hispanic population in the United States who also are black. In Miami, for example, nearly 30,000 residents identify themselves as both Cuban and black. They tend to be rejected by American-born blacks who identify them as Cuban and by other Cubans who identify them as black. The political processes in Dade County (metropolitan Miami) require representation of Cubans and of American-born blacks, but a Cuban black fulfills neither of those political requirements.

Another example of the demand for ethnic identification can be seen in the criteria for selecting members of the Cabinet of the president of the United States, for the selection of faculty in colleges and universities, and for the election of officers, executives, staff persons, and committee members in denominational systems.

A recent example of the pressure for ethnic identification came in the mid-1990s when the names of two dozen public schools in New Orleans were changed. The George Washington School, named for a slave owner who was the first president of the United States, was renamed the Dr. Charles Richard Drew Elementary School to honor a black surgeon who was the first director of the American Red Cross blood bank. The P. G. T. Beauregard Junior High School was renamed the Thurgood Marshall Middle School. The Robert E. Lee School was renamed the Ronald McNair School in honor of the second black astronaut.

Those who are ideologically committed to a completely integrated culture point to Bosnia, Guyana, Quebec, Trinidad and Tobago, South Africa, and the Congo as examples of how a strong emphasis on ethnic separation can lead to destructive adversarial relationships.

What is a valid assumption about the contemporary American culture? That the dominant trend is racial and cultural integration? Or that the dominant trend is ethnic separation?

Assume that you, the reader, are (1) a person with a western European ancestry, (2) an influential leader in a denomination in which at least 85 percent of today's adult members trace their ancestry back to western Europe, (3) ideologically committed to helping this become a truly multicultural denomination, and (4) a member of a special committee designing a strategy to turn that dream into reality.

If you are convinced the dominant contemporary trend is toward racial, ethnic, and cultural integration, you probably will urge that four of the central components of that strategy be (1) to encourage existing Anglo congregations to become multicultural churches; (2) to plant what from day one will be multicultural new churches; (3) to encourage every regional judicatory to become a multicultural organization with leaders deliberately drawn from a variety of racial, national, lingual, cultural, and ethnic heritages; and (4) to insist that every future pastor be trained for ministry in a theological school with a multicultural faculty and a multicultural student body, but one that originally was founded by and for people from a western European religious heritage. (Those with a deep commitment to full ethnic integration might insist that all Anglos preparing for the parish ministry receive their seminary training in a theological school that originally was founded to prepare Latinos or American-born blacks or Asians or Africans for the parish ministry.)

If, however, you are convinced that ethnic separation is the dominant theme today and that it also is the preference of most leaders in ethnic minority groups, you will not be surprised to learn that in several dozen regional judicatories affiliated with a predominantly white denomination (SBC, UMC, PCUSA, UCC, for example), the congregation with the largest average worship attendance is a monocultural ethnic minority church. You also are more likely to insist that the new strategy will emphasize (1) creating a large number and a broad variety of monocultural new churches; (2) encouraging the creation or emergence of bicultural congregations, but placing a relatively low priority on building multicultural congregations that include substantial numbers of adults from four or five or six different cultural heritages; (3) forming monocultural and nongeographical regional judicatories; and (4) creating a national network of new monocultural training centers that do not represent a western European heritage for preparing the next generation of parish pastors and program staff members.

For Anglos with a powerful ideological commitment to the full racial, cultural, and ethnic integration of society and also a strong attachment to a western European religious heritage, a different question surfaces. Should that strategy be designed on the basis of how the world should be, even if that slows the pace of reaching the goal of becoming a multicultural denomination? Or should that strategy affirm the trend toward ethnic separation as a fact of life in order to accelerate the pace of turning this into a multicultural denomination?

Do you see the trend away from racial integration and toward ethnic separation a sign of hope or a cause of despair? The answer will be influenced by your values, goals, and criteria for evaluation.

From Minority to Majority

For many years the custom at First Church was for the program staff to meet for two hours nearly every Tuesday morning. In 1963 that group included the senior minister, two associate ministers, the director of Christian education, the full-time choir director, the part-time organist, the semi-retired part-time minister of pastoral care, the church business administrator, and the pastor's secretary. Seven of the nine people in the room were male and two were female. All but two were full-time.

The passage of time has brought a significant increase in the size of First Church, and it now averages 1,135 at worship compared to 785 in 1963. Today weekly staff meetings are usually limited to five full-time people: the senior minister, the executive pastor, the pastor's administrative assistant, the program director, and the director of the learning community who also is one of the two regular weekly preachers. Together they constitute the leadership team in a new staff configuration designed to function as a team of teams.

These five plus three other full-time staff members plus eighteen part-time staffers attend a monthly two-hour gathering. In addition to those five who meet together on a regular weekly schedule, this monthly meeting includes the minister of prayer, the minister of health, the minister of pastoral care, a retired physician, the three full-time and four part-time team leaders for seven specialized areas of ministry (ministries with families with very young children, families that include elementary-school-age children, families that include middle school children, families that include high-school-age youth, young adults, mature adults, and newlyweds), the director of communications, the minister of missions (who also is a full-time campus minister at the nearby university), the four leaders of the four worship teams for the four weekly worship services (Saturday evening, early Sunday morning, late Sunday morning, and "The Good News at Six O'clock" Sunday evening), the media specialist, the minister of small groups, the minister of community outreach, and the part-time organist (who plays at the early Sunday morning service and at weddings and funerals).

Three of those eight full-time staffers and six of the eighteen part-time people in the room are male. Incidentally, twelve of those eighteen part-time program staff members are either fully or partially retired from secular employment.

When compared to the middle third of the twentieth century, women are far more numerous as (1) members of the governing board of congregations, (2) students in theological schools, (3) pastors of small churches, (4) teachers and administrators in Christian day schools, (5) program staff members of very large congregations, (6) staff members or executives in both regional judicatories and national denominational agencies, (7) members of the faculty or administrators of theological schools, (8) associate ministers in larger congregations, (9) staff members of parachurch organizations, (10) contributors to religious periodicals and religion editors for metropolitan newspapers, (11) pastoral counselors, and (12) members of a pastoral nominating or call committee.

Thanks largely to Title IX, the number of high school girls participating in competitive sports increased sevenfold between 1970 and 1998. The proportion of women engaged in the practices of medicine, law, politics, and dentistry also has increased dramatically since 1970.

In several annual conferences in the United Methodist Church, the majority of the newly ordained ministers since 1990 have been women, many of whom are second-career candidates.

Very, very few women are serving as mission developers of new missions or as senior pastors of very large congregations, but at least 98 percent of all ministers of prayer and 99 percent of all ministers of health (sometimes called parish nurses) are female, and a rapidly increasing proportion of church business administrators and executive pastors are women.

This reduction of the limitations placed on the role of women represents one of the half-dozen most significant changes in the context for ministry of the last half of the twentieth century. The twenty-first century will determine whether the professional practices of ministry, dentistry, membership in state legislatures and city councils, service as public defenders, and counseling become predominantly female vocations.

A look at the other side of the street reveals (1) the number of Roman Catholic nuns in the United States has decreased from approximately 180,000 in 1965 to 87,000 in 1998, (2) a survey conducted by the *Los Angeles Times* in 1994 reported that only 3 percent of all American nuns were under age 40, (3) 38 percent of those 87,000 nuns in 1998 already had celebrated their 71st birthday, (4) a growing number of small Roman Catholic parishes now are being served by a nun as the resident pastor, and (5) the number of Roman Catholic women who have earned the Master of Divinity degree and expect eventually to be ordained as priests keeps growing year after year.

From Vertical to Horizontal

What is the most widely discussed point of discontinuity that younger generations have brought to the business world, to military organizations, to higher education, to professional sports, to the entertainment industry, and to the American political scene?

One answer could be a resistance to the traditional hierarchical structures. Younger generations appear to be more comfortable with institutions that operate with a flatter organizational structure. Among the exceptions to that generalization are the institutions designed to deliver health-care services; several Christian bodies that are seeking to perpetuate a western religious heritage with a constituency consisting largely of the third, fourth, fifth, and sixth generations of American-born adults; and a shrinking number of college and university presidents.

Several of the consequences of this change are discussed elsewhere, including the expanded ministry of the laity, the new opportunities for women in ministry, the shift to a consumer orientation, new staff configurations in the larger churches, ministries with new generations of teenagers, the shift from passive to participatory worship, and the redefinition of the leadership styles of pastors.

Three other consequences merit a word here. The most widespread can be seen in the congregation that for years has been growing older and smaller. The new goal is to reach younger families and to grow larger. That usually requires many changes. One of the most difficult is to transform the role of the governing board from a permission-withholding body to a new role of challenging people to do what they know they cannot do.

A second is in financing the life and ministries of denominational systems. Instead of depending on the old hierarchical structure to secure undesignated dollars from member congregations, the successor plan calls for identifying and enlisting the support of partners. These partners in ministry may be individuals, family foundations, congregations, corporations, governmental agencies, larger foundations, or other philanthropic and religious organizations.

The old system worked with a reasonable degree of effectiveness in the 1950s and 1960s for councils of churches, the Roman Catholic Church, several of the mainline Protestant denominations, labor unions, political parties, and other voluntary associations. The central organization could depend on member contributions for adequate to generous financial support. The gradual disappearance of the generations born before World War II has undermined that old reliable system of financing hierarchical institutions.

Younger generations, plus some converts from older generations, are more comfortable with a new approach. That new approach usually includes these seven characteristics: (1) a flatter organizational structure; (2) shared decision making; (3) a recognition that every institution has to earn and re-earn the trust and confidence of its constituency; (4) instead of attempting to rally people and organizations to contribute undesignated dollars as a product of their loyalty to that institution and/or membership, the process calls for building partnerships in formulating goals, establishing priorities, and designing action plans; (5) the motivation for financial support is to support a clearly defined cause and/or to implement a precisely defined action plan; (6) the self-fulfilling prophecy that a significant amount of the total financial support will come from individuals who are not members of that organization but who believe in the cause; and (7) accurate, comprehensive, and regular reporting to the donors of what has been accomplished because of their financial support. The old system reprimanded members who did not support the central organization. The new system thanks donors for their gifts.

A third and overlapping consequence of this shift from vertical to horizontal organizational structures is the obsolescence of several of the old reliable methods of motivating people. Fear, guilt, institutional loyalty, the threat of recriminations, and duty are less effective than they were in the 1950s.

The replacement concepts include love, trust, participation, excitement, the attractiveness of the cause, partnerships, interpersonal relationships, and challenges. Paralleling this change, younger generations also have introduced another revolutionary point of discontinuity with the past.

From Institutions to Individuals

For the first half of the twentieth century, Americans were taught to trust institutions. Examples include the confidence that the New Deal could combat the Great Depression; that theological seminaries and university-related divinity schools were the best places to prepare future generations of parish pastors; that national brand names guaranteed the consumer a high-quality product; that the partnership of the schools of agriculture, the land-grant universities, and the United States Department of Agriculture could greatly improve the practice of agriculture; that membership in the League of Nations—and later the United Nations—was the best way to prevent another world war; that political parties could and should be trusted to nominate the best candidates for the presidency of the United States; that national denominational systems could and should be trusted to produce the resources needed by congregations affiliated with that denomination; that the United States State Department could be trusted to determine the best approach on American foreign policy; that hospitals were places that cured people; that big publishing houses were the best systems for publishing and selling books; that the most prudent and productive way for a congregation to be engaged in both foreign and home missions was to send money and candidates for endorsement as career missionaries to denominational headquarters; that university schools of education could be trusted to pioneer the best ways to train public school teachers; and that institutions controlled by white people could be trusted to decide what would be best for black people.

The Civil Rights movement of the 1950s and the anti–Vietnam War protests of the 1960s marked the beginning of an era that taught younger generations of Americans to distrust institutions. This new allegiance to movements replaced the old loyalty to institutions, including loyalty to governmental institutions. The next stage was the shift from an allegiance to movements to a participation in networks, which is discussed in the next section. The mid-1990s brought the arrival of a new era. Literally millions of individuals are turning to one another as they seek to deal with personal, family, and societal concerns. Spontaneity has replaced long-term loyalty.

Earlier generations felt their personal needs were being fulfilled by joining a lodge, a service club, a veterans' organization, a religious congregation, a women's missionary group, a denomination, a bowling team, a civic organization, a political post, or some similar institution.

The younger generations of today feel a need to bond with other individuals who are experiencing the same personal needs.

This change in the American culture created five alternatives for people.

1. Deny this has happened and try to operate on the assumption that everyone still trusts large institutions.

2. Conclude that neither institutions nor individuals can be trusted and live in a world of despair and chaos.

3. Redefine one's perception of reality and operate on the assumption that while it may not always be prudent to trust large institutions, individuals who earn your trust and confidence can be relied on to be responsive to your needs.

4. Express your confidence only in those institutions and individuals who (a) accept the responsibility to earn and re-earn your trust and (b) by their performance prove that they can be trusted.

5. Create a new social network of people in which the members bond together on the basis of neighbor-centered love, common concerns, and mutual support.

Perhaps the most highly visible example of this expression of the generation gap in the churches is expressed between the loyal members of the traditional women's missionary organization and the women who are participating in one or more components of the women's ministries described in the first chapter.

Among the other consequences of this change are these. Presidential candidates are now chosen by the voters in primary elections, and that choice is confirmed by party conventions. Fewer dollars are being sent to denominational headquarters as congregations become more directly engaged in both worldwide missions and local outreach ministries. The newly arrived pastor has to earn and re-earn the trust and confidence of the parishioners. A large proportion of the founding pastors of large and rapidly growing congregations are individuals who never graduated from seminary. The crucial vote of approval for a proposed building program comes from the results of the capital funds campaign rather than from a meeting of the governing board. Younger generations are choosing a church home on the basis of the personality, the belief system, the teaching, and the preaching of the pastor, rather than in response to the denominational affiliation of that congregation.

Younger candidates for ordination are choosing a theological school on the basis of finding fellow students with whom they have much in common rather than on the basis of the academic reputation or denominational affiliation of that seminary.

Denominational staff persons working directly with congregations have to earn and re-earn the trust of the members rather than rely on the credibility of a denominational affiliation. Large-scale donors are more likely to be motivated by the attractiveness of the cause and the persuasiveness of the messenger representing that cause than by the institutional affiliation of that messenger. Candidates for a vacant staff position are more likely to be evaluated on the basis of character, Christian commitment, competence, experience, and skills in interpersonal relationships rather than by credentials from academic or denominational institutions or membership on various institutional governing boards. A rapidly growing number of parents are choosing to educate their children at home rather than to enroll them in a public or private school. A proposal for a national health-care system died when it was discovered people trusted doctors more than they trusted governmental institutions. Pastorates are becoming longer because (a) it takes longer for that new pastor to enjoy the level of trust that formerly was granted to the occupant of that office but now must be earned, and (b) frequent pastoral changes tend to undermine the level of trust in the position of pastor. An increasing number of senior pastors of very large and denominationally affiliated congregations are being criticized for their apparent lack of interest in supporting the goals of that denomination.

From a long-term perspective, one of the most significant consequences is the creation of ad hoc networks. An increasing proportion of younger adults choose to *participate* in a network rather than to *join* an institution.

A second consequence can be summarized in a single question: What motivates people to leave the comfort of home and the security of their job to attend a mass meeting? In the 1960s and 1970s it was relatively easy to motivate people born in the 1925–50 era to participate in protest marches. These marches rallied people together in support of a cause. Examples include the civil rights marches and the anti–Vietnam War protests. Among the points of commonality were (1) an outward focus on public policy, (2) calls for changes in governmental policies, (3) a shared ideological perspective on the world, and (4) large numbers of participants who were encouraged to participate as a result of their membership in a larger institution (congregation, denomination, labor union, civil rights organization, university, peace movement, and the like).

The 1990s brought the 1995 Million Man March led by Minister Louis Farrakhan, the 1997 Promise Keepers "Stand in the Gap" rally, and the 1997 rally in Philadelphia of hundreds of thousands of women of African ancestry. Among the points of commonality among all three, to varying degrees, were (1) self-improvement, (2) the reinforcement of a sense of brotherhood or sisterhood, (3) spiritual revival, (4) self-esteem, (5) the accepting and fulfilling of one's personal responsibilities, especially husbands and fathers, (6) the looking inward on one's own resources rather than expecting government to solve the problems, (7) a desire to bond with others who feel the same inner needs, and (8) little emphasis on one's relationships to larger institutions.

A third long-term consequence is the emergence of teams. These team members *work* for an institution (a major league baseball team or an automobile company or a medical clinic or a huge law firm or a church or a governmental agency or a public school system), but they *belong* to their team. Their primary loyalty is to their team. Their secondary loyalty is to the cause they seek to advance (win that ball game or heal that patient or challenge that student to do better). A distant third loyalty may be to the institution that provides that regular paycheck.

How has this erosion of trust in large institutions affected your congregation and your relationships with your denomination?

From Superstar to Teams

The sixty-nine-year-old senior minister at First Church had announced he was preparing to retire after a thirty-five-year pastorate. His tenure had seen the worship attendance climb from an average of two hundred and twenty-five to slightly over fourteen hundred. During those three and one-half decades First Church had relocated its meeting place and completed four large building programs.

About a year before the big retirement banquet designed to honor this pastor's ministry, a half-dozen influential lay leaders began to meet informally. Their self-assigned task was to begin the process of searching for a successor. By the end of their fifth meeting, they had agreed they had five responsibilities.

1. To assemble a special ad hoc task force that would be responsible for that banquet.

2. To assemble another special task force that would collect the money for a farewell gift for this senior minister and his wife.

3. To aggressively build a list of potential candidates to succeed this gifted, energetic, visionary, and popular minister who also was a superb preacher, an entrepreneurial leader, and a loving shepherd.

4. To begin the process of terminating the employment of two long-tenured staff members who had many friends and supporters among the members, but who also were exceptionally ineffective.

5. To gently inform all the other program staff members that, while their work was greatly appreciated, they would be expected to submit an undated letter of resignation to the new senior minister on the first day that person began work. "We hope the new senior minister will tear up that letter, but a new senior minister has a right to build a new staff," was the explanation for this agenda item.

The year was 1985.

* * *

Recently the forty-nine-year-old senior minister at Trinity Church called together a dozen of the most knowledgeable, deeply committed, widely influential, and supportive volunteer leaders in this congregation that was averaging close to a thousand at worship.

"Three months ago I attended the memorial service for one of my closest friends in the ministry," began this senior minister. "He was killed in an automobile accident a month before his fiftieth birthday. He had served as the founding pastor of that congregation nineteen years ago. They now average about eighteen hundred at worship. After the service a couple of the ministers on the staff whom I've known for years asked for some time to talk with me. A few days ago they scheduled a conference telephone call that included three of their key lay leaders."

"They want you to come and be their new senior minister?" interrupted one of the men.

"No, that's not the issue," replied this pastor. "They wanted to talk about two other concerns. First, they realized they were without a plan of succession. They had lost their leader. They had never gone through the process of succession. Second, they asked me to suggest some names of potential successors."

"What's that got to do with us?" asked another member of this ad hoc group. "Do they expect us to give them some names?"

"No, I didn't ask you to meet to solve their problem," continued this pastor. "I asked you to meet this evening to talk about how we can avoid the problem they are facing. They're looking for a superstar preacher to come in and follow my friend. That is an impossible task. He spent nineteen years building relationships with people in that congregation. No one can come in and fill that hole. The parallel issue we are faced with here is that we also lack a plan of succession. I had always assumed that I would be here for another fifteen or twenty years, but I now realize life is uncertain. I want to talk with you about designing a plan of succession in case something should happen to me."

The year was 1998.

* * *

"Nine years ago we lost two of our very best staff members," explained the fifty-two-year-old head of the leadership team at Bethany Church. "One was our minister of pastoral care who had a sudden heart attack and died the next day at age sixty-three. A week earlier our director of Christian education had retired after nearly thirty years on staff. As we began our search to replace them, we discovered the most promising younger potential candidates were turning us down. One of the reasons several offered was they were involved in team ministries where they were, and they weren't interested in leaving that type of staff configuration for what we offered. At the time, our program staff consisted of five full-time positions—senior minister, associate minister, director of Christian education, minister of pastoral care, and minister of music. At age forty-three, I was the newest and youngest member of the staff. When I arrived, I had accepted that staff configuration without question. It resembled the staff of the church I had left where I was the senior associate minister."

"What is your present staff configuration now?" inquired the senior minister from Trinity Church who had come to study other models.

"We are now a team of teams organized around ministry rather than around individual staff specialties. Most of our ministry teams include three to fifteen lay volunteers plus one or two or three paid staff members. For example, our pastoral care team includes one pastor, who also serves on two other teams, our half-time minister of wellness, our quarter-time minister of prayer, three retired nurses, a retired physician, and seven volunteers who have been trained as Stephen Ministers. We now have five worship teams, one for each of our five weekend worship experiences, and each includes two part-time specialists plus our full-time media specialist plus five to twelve volunteers. We have one team that focuses on families that include expectant mothers or babies newborn through age three. That team includes two part-time musicians and a grandmother who is our part-time specialist in early childhood development plus a part-time pediatric nurse. Currently I am the head of our leadership team that also includes our executive pastor, our program director, and two other preachers. Altogether we have eight full-time and thirty-six part-time people on our program staff."

"What's happened since you began to build this new staff configuration?" asked the visiting pastor.

"Among the changes are these seven," came the reply. "First, our average worship attendance has nearly tripled from slightly under six hundred to about seventeen hundred. Second, the median age of our confirmed membership has dropped from fifty-seven years to thirty-nine. Third, I was the youngest person on the payroll nine years ago, and now I'm the fourth oldest. Fourth, we now have a staff composed largely of relatively young, high-energy, creative, future-oriented, and highly skilled part-time specialists. Fifth, we've been able to eliminate nearly all the old standing committees that used to meet monthly. Today we have only two stand-ing committees, one on property and one on finances. The successors to those people who used to serve on standing committees now serve on ministry teams or on single-purpose ad hoc ministry task forces. Sixth, during the first two or three years of making these changes, we lost the pre-dictable thirty families, some of whom had been members here for many, many years. Finally, when we designed our last building program, we constructed a new office wing. It includes only three one-person offices—one for me, one for the executive pastor, and one for the program director. In addition, we have nine large rooms for teams. The typical room has cubicles for three to six paid staff members plus three or four desks for volunteers, each with its own tele-phone, plus cabinets, counters, tables, and storage cabinets."

One of the motivating forces behind this shift from staffing individual empires to building teams has been the experiences of lay volunteers in the churches who have worked as part of a team in an elementary school or in the corporate world or in the nonprofit sector. Overlapping that is the preference of a large proportion of the most talented people born after 1955 who prefer to work as part of a team, rather than alone.

One consequence is that more and more larger congrega-tions are creating a new staff configuration built around the concept of a team of teams.[4]

A second consequence is that this has turned out to be a creative and productive response to the new emphasis on the ministry of the laity described in the first chapter.

A third consequence is the revolution in the organiza-tional structure of congregations. The old structures usually were designed to centralize control in the governing board. This new staff configuration calls for organizing both paid staff and lay volunteers around ministry and missions, rather than around control.

The most widely ignored consequence concerns the career path of the next generation of parish pastors.

One design calls for them first to graduate from a theological school in which the faculty models the role of the individual expert. The reward system there reinforces the value of individual performance, such as publishing an award-winning scholarly monograph or lecturing at scholarly gatherings and denominational events. The next stage often calls for either serving as the only full-time paid person on the staff of a small or middle-sized congregation or serving a postseminary apprenticeship as a generalist on the staff of a larger congregation for a few years before departing to become the pastor "of my own church."

The second design challenges the believer, who is a member of a large congregation, first to become a disciple of Jesus Christ. Following that transformation, this person becomes a volunteer on a ministry team. Subsequently, several of these volunteers are called to serve as part-time paid members of a ministry team in that congregation. Eventually a small percentage of these members of a ministry team become convinced they have been called by God to full-time Christian ministry. Some of them conclude that a seminary degree and ordination is a requirement to fulfill that call. They continue to work on a ministry team, either part-time or full-time, while fulfilling the academic requirements for that degree and ordination. They may commute to a seminary campus or they may take most or all of those classes in a classroom in the building housing the congregation they serve.

Does this basic trend of creating mission teams of paid staff and lay volunteers rank high on your list of signs of hope? Which design do you believe will be most effective in producing the ordained members of ministry teams in 2025? In producing the lay volunteers for those ministry teams?

From Generalist to Specialist ╼

Overlapping that preference to serve as a member of a team, rather than as a generalist or as a solo performer, younger generations also are responding to the societal demand for specialists. The sixty-nine-year-old physician spent a satisfying career as a general practitioner. His daughter, who also is a physician, has decided to specialize in heart surgery. Similar intergenerational patterns can be seen in the practice of law, in real estate, in farming, in education, in banking, in electronics, in automobile repair, and in journalism.

The parallel trend in the churches is that the smaller congregations are being priced out of the market for the full-time and fully credentialed pastors who serve as generalists, and the larger congregations are seeking staff, both lay and ordained, with a high level of competence in a narrowly specialized area of ministry. Examples include ministries with (1) families that include very young children, (2) developmentally disabled adults, (3) the recently divorced, (4) mature adults, (5) blended families, (6) never-married adults born after 1970, (7) couples who have adopted a child born in another culture, (8) older adults living alone, (9) couples in an intercultural marriage, (10) adults with AIDS, (11) families that include teenagers, (12) small groups, (13) families with the husband and father in jail or prison, (14) newly engaged couples, and (15) single parents.

Other examples include the minister of recreation, the church nurse, the webmaster, the minister of prayer, the leader of a worship team, the media specialist, and the minister of missions.

Is it reasonable to expect theological schools to be able to mobilize the resources required to train these and other specialists in ministries? Or should congregations be looking to other sources, such as the teaching churches, to train the specialists for the twenty-first century? Or could this be a partnership between teaching churches and theological schools?

This growing demand for highly skilled specialists, plus the changes in the national labor market, have created another trend that also is being pioneered largely by younger adults.

From Full-time to Part-time

The seminary student looking forward to a full-time career in the parish ministry may discover recent changes in the American labor force should be near the top of this list of points of discontinuity with the past. Through the 1950s most adults worked in a full-time job, often with the same employer, until retirement.

In recent years, the number of part-time jobs has been increasing from three million in 1960 to nearly eight million in 1997. This was a widely publicized issue in the strike by the Teamsters Union against the United Parcel Service in mid-1997. It is an issue of equal concern to the growing number of adults who hold the Ph.D. degree and want to teach. The best many can find is three concurrent part-time teaching positions in three different institutions of higher education. Together those three part-time jobs produce one modest compensation package—but without the promise of eventual tenure.

Add to that trend the growing demand for specialized skills and the fact that the cost of providing person-centered services is increasing faster than the increase in the income levels of the population. One consequence is an increase in part-time jobs in the delivery of health-care services, in elementary and high schools, in the practice of law, and in the parish ministry.

The most significant example of this trend in the churches

is the large and growing congregation that clearly is competitive in reaching, attracting, and serving younger generations. Forty years ago most of the staff were full-time. Today half of the custodial staff and most of the program staff are part-time. In 1955 a church could be competitive with a staff of full-time generalists. Today being competitive requires several part-time, highly skilled specialists.

For many of these part-time specialists, joining the staff of this large congregation was the third or fourth career change since graduation from high school—and they may experience two or three more career changes before retirement.

Another facet of this trend is the gradual shrinkage in the number of congregations averaging fewer than a hundred at worship that can both economically afford and also justify, in terms of a challenging work load, a full-time and fully credentialed resident pastor. In a few wealthy denominations, the day of reckoning can be postponed by increasing the denominational subsidies for pastors. In most traditions, however, the trend already is apparent and is represented by the estimated 100,000 bivocational ministers, retirees, and laypersons now serving small churches.

In the pre-1975 era there was still widespread support for another alternative in providing ministerial leadership for smaller congregations. This was to create a full-time compensation package by asking one minister to serve two or three congregations concurrently. Sometimes this meant one minister would be serving congregations from two different denominational traditions.

All too often this arrangement produced (1) short pastorates and/or (2) a maintenance approach to ministry (which was more acceptable before the ecclesiastical scene became so highly competitive) and/or (3) the merging of congregations as younger generations refused to affirm and support this strategy and/or (4) the closing of thousands of churches and/or (5) the decision by congregational leaders that they preferred "our own" long-tenured bivocational minister to sharing a short-tenured full-time minister with one or two or three rivals for that pastor's affections.

Finally, in the 1950s and 1960s theological schools sought full-time scholars as they built their faculty. The current trend is in the direction of seeking successful practitioners who can teach on a part-time basis while continuing to serve in the parish ministry.

These part-time faculty members are modeling for their students the merits and satisfactions that can accompany two part-time vocations. That is a radically different model than was presented in past years by the world-famous scholar who earned a living teaching in a theological school.

Which of these patterns of employment do you expect will be the growing model in the twenty-first century?

1. The full-time seminary professor?

2. The practitioner of ministry who teaches on a part-time basis?

3. The bivocational minister with a full-time secular job who also serves as the long-tenured pastor of a small congregation?

4. The full-time minister who serves two or three small congregations concurrently?

5. The full-time generalist on the program staff of the very large church?

6. The part-time specialist on the program staff of the very large church?

7. The full-time generalist on the program staff of the regional judicatory?

8. The part-time specialist on the program staff of the regional judicatory?

9. The congregation or regional judicatory that contracts with an outside agency for the services of highly skilled specialists?

From Movements to Networks

The improvements in transportation and communication, the affluence of the last half of the twentieth century, and other forces have fostered the replacement of the neighborhood congregation by the regional church. Similar changes have produced new alternatives as individuals contemplate how they will invest their discretionary time and energy plus their hopes for making this a better world. One alternative was to invest in a single-issue movement such as the labor movement, the Civil Rights movement, the feminist movement, the ecumenical movement, the peace movement, or the movement to reform the denominational system.

The 1980s brought the emergence of what for many is a highly attractive alternative investment of personal resources. This is to help pioneer a network of individuals who share many of the same responsibilities, challenges, frustrations, opportunities, and dreams. One of the motivations for participating in one of these ad hoc networks is the interpersonal relationships that come with the creation of these homogeneous clusters. These clusters contrast with the old pattern that linked people together by employer or place of employment or institutional ties. They had failed to provide the personal fulfillment or the satisfactions sought by many younger adults. A second factor is that the key word in networks is not *joining,* but rather *participating.* A third motivation is that the best networks nurture and feed; they do not require a person to be willing to be exploited. The number one national and international example of this is the "chat rooms" on the Internet.

In the business world, one of the great success stories is Texas Instruments, Inc. Their marketing strategy for selling the TI-81 graphing calculator relies heavily on networks of twelve to twenty teachers. Each group is served by a TI project manager. Through these networks, TI trains about three hundred teachers annually who instruct other teachers on the use of calculators in school classrooms. Since TI calculators are used in these training sessions, it is not surprising that the teachers encourage their own school districts to purchase TI products.

The number one ecclesiastical example of this trend toward networking can be traced back to the 1960s when senior pastors of very large congregations began to gather in informal sessions to be stimulated, challenged, and spiritually fed as well as vocationally nurtured. The big fringe benefit was the opportunity to meet and make friends with peers, with people who shared the same concerns. Lutherans, Baptists, Methodists, members of the United Church of Christ, and Presbyterians were among the earliest participants in these ad hoc networks of senior pastors of large congregations.

In the mid-1980s the newly created Leadership Network based in Tyler, Texas, and now headquartered in Dallas, brought together senior pastors of both independent and denominationally affiliated congregations. The Alban Institute also has nurtured the creation of these ad hoc networks.

Individuals *join* movements. They *participate* in networks. A movement is created to advance a cause. A network comes into existence to fulfill the shared needs of a group of people. Movements enlist people in support of a cause. Networks gather people around a common agenda. Movements need constituents to feed and water the cause. Networks feed and water the constituents. Movements focus on a single and clearly identified agenda. Networks create agendas for tomorrow. Movements thrive in relationship to the skill and charisma of their leaders. Networks thrive on the interaction of their participants. Movements are threatened when someone introduces a new and potentially divisive agenda. (The debate about abortion undermined the interfaith civil rights movements of the 1950s and 1960s.) Networks are stimulated by the introduction of new and controversial subjects. Movements are sustained by advancing the cause. Networks are sustained by the personal and professional growth of the participants. Movements attract ideologically compatible people. Networks attract professionally compatible people who may differ greatly from one another ideologically. Movements seek to create a better world. Networks seek to create a better life for the participants.

One of the revolutionary changes in the religious world began to become more common in the 1960s and blossomed in the 1990s. The old pattern tended to build intercongregational partnerships on the basis of weaknesses. Perhaps the most common example was the circuit or yoked field. This called for two or three or more small congregations, each with limited resources, to be linked together to be served by one pastor. No one of these congregations had the financial resources required for a full-time and fully credentialed resident pastor. Whether the primary goal was to provide limited ministerial leadership to each congregation or to provide full-time jobs for the clergy, the result was the same. In most cases this arrangement not only affirmed and perpetuated weakness, it also placed a low ceiling on the possibilities for the future. Frequently this also turned out to be a useful interim step in a longer process of closing churches.

A recent urban parallel has been to merge two or three or more small, struggling, numerically shrinking, and weak congregations in the central city. The operational assumption appears to be that weakness plus terminal illness plus weakness plus despair can be combined to equal strength, health, and vitality. More often than not, this turns out to be an arrangement to buy time until someone else arrives to receive the blame for closing churches.

The revolutionary change often is expressed in one of two

forms. One is to link weakness to strength. One example is the strong and vital high expectation "missionary church" in the county-seat town that enlists and trains five to thirty lay ministers. Some work alone, while others work in teams. The network consists of that one missionary church with an abundance of resources and three to twenty small congregations within a thirty-mile radius, each with limited resources. Those lay ministers and leadership teams provide part-time preachers and leaders for those small congregations that can neither afford nor justify a full-time resident pastor. When the leaders of a particular congregation decide to raise the self-imposed ceiling, that missionary church can provide the needed outside, skilled, experienced, and committed lay leadership required to help make that happen.

The more common expression of this approach to networking is to link strength to strength. These three strong congregations form a network to plant one new mission every other year. These five strong, creative, and venturesome congregations create a network that designs and offers one major teaching event annually for congregational leaders who seek to learn from others. These three congregations create a network of volunteers to expand the ministry of an inner-city community center. These seven middle-sized congregations create a network of volunteers who construct one Habitat for Humanity house every year. That network of five congregations is designed to help volunteers and staff from each church to learn from one another as each launches its first off-campus ministry. By year four, volunteers from Church A are working with volunteers from seven other congregations in a new off-campus ministry being launched by Church E. Leaders in that network come from twelve churches in seven cities—each is the home of both the state capital and the original state university—to learn from one another how to do ministry in that unique environment. That network of five congregations is organized around the goal of creating one new worshiping community composed largely of recent high school graduates. That network of fifteen congregations came into existence to design, build, and operate a financially self-supporting home for developmentally disabled adults.

In addition to these networks composed of congregations, scores of networks have been created for ministers of music, Christian educators, senior ministers of large churches, divorced fathers, pastors of rural churches, single mothers, ministers of missions, couples who have adopted a child of a different race or nationality, interim ministers, church organists, executive pastors, associate ministers, church nurses, pastors who have been fired by their congregation, ministers of prayer, church business administrators, and dozens of other specialties. Most cut across denominational lines and include persons from independent churches.

Networks that welcome irregular participation are replacing classes that called for regular attendance. Networks of like-minded people or of congregations with similar missional goals are replacing geographically defined denominationally based clusters of congregations. Networks of eager learners are replacing standing committees in many organizations. Networks of teenagers are replacing the old congregationally based youth groups—but that is another story.

How do you evaluate this trend? Is the emergence of a variety of networks among the churches a sign of hope? Or a cause for despair?

From Family to Peers

Those of us who were reared on a farm spent most of our formative years in a world owned and operated by adults. The relatively small public schools offered students a variety of opportunities, often for three or four years, for close personal contact with one teacher who also served as a respected adult role model. During the summer, teenagers worked in the fields and the barns alongside adults.

All across the continent high school graduates entered the labor force by working alongside adults, many of whom were ten, twenty, thirty, or forty years older. These young people were socialized into the culture by continuing, long-term, and close contact with adult mentors.

Walk in the typical fast-food restaurant today and, with one or two exceptions, the work force consists entirely of teenagers.

Stephanie Coontz reports that in 1940, 60 percent of employed adolescents worked in traditional workplaces alongside adults who taught them both work and social skills that would benefit them for years. By 1980 that proportion had dropped to 14 percent.[5]

For the past quarter century the trend has been to socialize young people in a culture dominated by their peers, not by respected older adults.

Whether that is good or bad is another question. One result, however, is that intergenerational culture no longer is available to most young people to transmit either moral values or traditional standards of ethical behavior from one generation to the next. Should the schools be expected to do this? Or parents? Or the churches? Or should we expect that each generation will invent its own code of moral values and its own standards of ethical behavior? Or is that the responsibility of employers?

Some readers may respond, "So what?" to this issue. One answer to that question came in 1997 with a research study that indicated that teenagers who reported feeling close to their parents or other respected adults were the least likely to engage in any of the high-risk behaviors studied, such as sexual intercourse or the use of drugs, alcohol, and tobacco. It also indicated that students who felt their teachers cared for them were less likely to engage in high-risk behavior.[6]

While at least one-half of today's adolescents are influenced to a far greater degree by their peers than by respected older adults, that may not be the ideal road into the twenty-first century.

An alternative that began to be adopted by a growing number of congregations goes back to the early 1980s. That called for scrapping the traditional approach to youth ministries that focused on teenagers and replacing it with a package of ministries that focused on families that included teenagers.

Overlapping the trend toward peer relationships among teenagers is another point of discontinuity with the past. This is the sharp increase in the number of adults in their twenties who are not living with either their parents or their spouse. One father commented, "For the first time in human history, mature women by the tens of thousands live the entire decade of their twenties—their most fertile years—neither in the homes of their fathers nor in the homes of their husbands." This aging university professor goes on to lift up the need to call for religious institutions to help restore a more supportive national climate for marriage.[7]

That is not an easy challenge! In the 1950s pastors served within a societal context that still endorsed and supported marriage. Today the culture is far less supportive of marriage.[8]

The singles group of 1960, where never-married adults in their mid- and late twenties and early thirties came to meet their future spouse, frequently has evolved into a group of formerly married adults in their forties and fifties.

Building a singles ministry with people born in the 1970s is far more difficult than it was in the 1960s with people born in the 1930s. Among the high-skill assignments given to the church today are (1) the ministry with young adults that includes never-married individuals and childless couples; (2) the ministry with newly engaged couples; (3) the adult Sunday school class for newlyweds and couples about to be married; (4) the ministry with adults in the midst of a traumatic divorce experience; (5) the ministry with teenagers who deeply resent the remarriage of the divorced or widowed parent with whom they have been living for several years; (6) the young adults who are now ready to deal with the psychological scars inflicted on them by the divorce of their parents ten to twenty years earlier; (7) the premarital counseling with the couple, both of whom have been married before, who are about to embark on a new marriage (in four out of ten weddings, one or both parties had been married previously); (8) the ministry with children in single-parent homes; (9) the ministry with youth from single-parent homes; (10) the ministry with the newly blended families that include children from two previous marriages; (11) the ministry with newlyweds who spent ten to fifteen years as single adults before their first marriage; and (12) the ministry with grandparents who unexpectedly are rearing their parentless grandchildren.

That is a BIG assignment for the ordained generalist serving a congregation that averages 125 at worship!

The second half of this same change in the cultural context for ministry begins earlier in life. As recently as the 1950s, teenagers looked to adults for wisdom, advice, experience, and counsel.

For most of today's youth the two most influential forces on their decision-making processes are either (a) peers and television or (b) television and their peers. By the time this book is published, that list may have changed to peers, the Internet, and television.

The adult volunteer who wants to recreate the youth program she or he experienced as a teenager usually will find only 10 to 35 percent of today's teenagers interested in that approach. This point of discontinuity with the past also complicates life for the thirty-five-year-old professional youth pastor and the forty-year-old campus minister.

Three common and simple illustrations of the fork-in-the-road questions posed by this trend can be stated in these terms.

1. Should we concentrate on a peer-led model for youth ministries here? Or should we create a model that will bring as many teenagers as possible into continuing relationships with several adults who (a) truly love teenagers, (b) are excellent models of an adult Christian, (c) will be able to earn the respect and admiration of teenagers, and (d) will be influential models of a healthy mature adult? Or should we conceptualize this as a package of ministries with families that include teenagers?

2. Should we seek to create a vocal choir of youth in grades 6-12? Or one in grades 6-9 and another in grades 10-12? Or should we invite all interested teenagers to be members of an intergenerational vocal group or an intergenerational band or orchestra or an intergenerational Bible study group?

3. When we staff ministries with teenagers, should we seek adults in their twenties? Or in their thirties? Or in their forties? Or as many as possible past age fifty?

Finally, for some the most threatening change comes out of the questions being raised about the traditional pedagogical model. That model called for adults to teach children. The twenty-five-year-old public-school teacher taught a class of fourth graders. The grandmother taught a children's class in Sunday school. The fifty-five-year-old full professor taught a seminar for graduate students in their twenties. The forty-year-old man coached the high school basketball team. Older people taught younger people.

One challenge to that model emerged many years ago when the cliché was heard, "Graduate students learn from one another." A second challenge came when the thirty-five-year-old seminary professor taught a course on urban ministries to a class that included several who chose the parish ministry as a second career, including the forty-five-year-old ex-principal of an inner-city high school, the forty-two-year-old former city planner, the fifty-year-old former emergency room nurse in a teaching hospital, and the black minister who was in his twentieth year as an inner-city pastor but only now had been able to afford to attend seminary.

Another challenge came from a research project at Stanford University that reported peer teaching was more effective in improving learning than was reducing class size or utilizing computer-aided instruction or increasing the time for direct adult-to-student instruction.

How has this new emphasis on peer relationships and peer teaching affected the ministry of your congregation?

From Passive to Active

During the 1930s children born in the previous decade collected stamps. Many of their children jog or engage in some other form of strenuous exercise weekly. Many of the boys born in the 1940s played Little League baseball, a game which calls for most of the players to spend most of their time standing in the field or sitting on a bench. Their children play soccer, a game which rarely allows anyone to be idle.

Americans spend less time reading the daily newspaper and more time reading the *American Woodworker* magazine, which increased its circulation fifteenfold to 330,000 between 1988 and 1998. Instead of collecting coins, a relatively passive hobby, many will spend $550 for a five-day class learning how to make a Windsor chair. Others will spend $395 for a two-and-one-half-day course learning the art of fly-fishing. Women engaged to be married formerly registered their preferences for such bridal gifts as china and silverware at the department store. Their daughters register their wish lists at stores selling exercise equipment or sports paraphernalia or garden supplies or construction tools.

In 1954 the twenty-seven-year-old husband and his twenty-four-year-old wife came to church to sit passively most of the time while the minister and the choir director led the congregation in the corporate worship of God. A few dozed, but most stayed awake for the whole hour. Forty-five years later this empty-nest couple attend the same church and rejoice in the continuity with the past. The names and faces have changed, but the new minister and the new choir director lead the congregation in what is largely a 1950s style of passive worship compatible with the radio era of the 1930s.

All of their four children are now in their forties. One is a pillar in a large, ten-year-old, independent, growing congregation organized around a participatory style of worship; the second does not go to church; the third recently joined a mainline Protestant congregation; and the fourth is a member of a charismatic church.

Three of this couple's six grandchildren are now adults. The oldest is married and an active member of a congregation organized around "contemporary" worship that is compatible with the television era. The second does not go to church. The third is an active member of a parachurch ministry at the state university.

As recently as the 1950s the country was well supplied with large adult Sunday school classes in which one person prepared and "presented" the lesson for that day. The forty- and fifty-year-olds of the day appreciated those classes. They went home nearly every week knowing they had learned something that enriched their life as a Christian.

Today's forty-year-old is more likely to prefer a class organized around a discussion format. These participants subsequently go out to lunch with some friends knowing that

(a) their point of view had been heard, (b) their understanding of what it means to be a disciple of Jesus Christ had been challenged and expanded, and (c) the time had come to consider moving from being an admirer of Jesus to becoming a fully devoted follower of the Christ.

While it is dangerous to push a cause-and-effect relationship, two parallel trends are clear. One is that an increasing proportion of the adult population has chosen a hobby that (a) demands strenuous physical involvement, (b) encourages an increasingly higher level of physical skill, and (c) tempts people to spend considerable money and time in structured learning experiences that challenge them to do what they know they cannot do.

The second, which is the central theme of this chapter, is that new generations bring a new context for ministry. One part of that new context is the large proportion of younger adults who prefer a participatory rather than a spectator approach to ministry. One expression of this is in the changes in worship. A second part is that younger generations tend to prefer to be challenged to be engaged in doing ministry rather than serving on standing committees or writing checks.

Do you identify this trend as a source of alarm? Or as a sign of hope?

From Improvement to Entertainment

"When I began my career as a pastor sixty years ago," recalled the eighty-three-year-old minister, "people came to church prepared to listen to the proclamation of God's holy Word. The preacher had the responsibility to proclaim the Word of God faithfully and obediently. The people came knowing they had the responsibility to listen. Today everyone assumes it is the responsibility of the preacher to grab and hold the attention of the people in the pews. Television has taught people to be irresponsible. The result is that what used to be the corporate worship of God has become entertainment. If their minister can't entertain them, they'll go to one of these superchurches that will. I'm glad I was able to retire when I did!"

This retired preacher entered the ministry in an era when the American culture assumed that (1) children went to school to learn; (2) Christians went to church to be inspired, enlightened, and motivated by listening to the sermon; (3) following adoption of the Production Code of 1930 (which was written by a Roman Catholic layman and a Jesuit priest), Hollywood would produce motion pictures that affirmed and reinforced traditional American middle-class values—this was most apparent during the 1940s when scores of movies celebrated the Allied role in World War II and exalted the role of the Roman Catholic priest; (4) college and university students were expected to do two hours of homework for every hour in the classroom; (5) the news report on the radio reported the news, sports, and a weather forecast; and (6) for most adults, shopping was a necessary chore, not an adventure.

That retired minister is right. The world he once knew has largely disappeared. Four of the skills required of the person who wants to forecast the weather as part of the local television news are (1) competence as an oral communicator, (2) an entertaining personality, (3) the ability to grab and hold the attention of the viewers, and (4) a reasonable level of competence in meteorology.

A recent evaluation by students of their teachers at the University of California at Berkeley placed a high value on entertainment skills. Most of the teachers who received high ratings from the students were described by comments such as these: "humorous, fun, and fair"; "tells lots of jokes, entertaining"; "fantastic sense of humor"; and "dry humor." Those who received low scores in these student evaluations often were described as "He really tends to ramble and he just does not hold my attention," "dull lecturer," and "difficult to stay awake."[9]

In 1995 Nathan Myhrvold, the chief technology officer for Microsoft, commented, "Our business is getting closer to entertainment every day."[10] A growing number of six-year-olds agree that computers are sources of entertainment.

That retired minister is right. The person seeking to communicate orally with a crowd has a far more difficult and demanding task today than was true in 1939 or 1959.

A persuasive argument can be made that the contemporary demand by the public to be entertained represents the most significant change in the context for ministry during the last third of the twentieth century.[11]

One group of critics points to the modern megachurch as the chief villain in this story. Others identify television as the number one villain. Those with a longer memory attribute the beginning of the fall from grace to motion pictures. More than a few contend the beginning of the end traces back to the days when courtship moved from the swing on the front porch to the back seat of the automobile and the drive-in movie theater.

More recently, the Mills Corporation of Arlington, Virginia, has transformed the role of shopping malls from centers for retail trade into a combination of (1) eating places designed as experiences that also serve food, such as the Rainforest Cafe, (2) a small zoo, (3) outlet stores, (4) motion-picture theaters, (5) an amusement park, and (6) specialty retail stores. Entertainment is the name of this game.

At least a few will argue that the decisive change came when evangelicals changed their stance from being predictable and vocal critics of entertainment as the work of the devil to building entertainment into worship and learning. They point to Billy Sunday and other revivalist preachers of that era as the first to legitimatize entertainment as an acceptable part of the effort to preach the gospel to the unsaved. A fair number contend that the decline in the political influence of the Roman Catholic Church that began in the 1950s has been a crucial factor.

For many mature adults the obvious villain is the combination of the new music and today's youth. Those mature adults can recall when they went to a concert or tuned in the radio or turned on a record player and listened to classical music. The youth of today apparently need to hear music when they are mowing the lawn or driving an automobile or walking down the street or riding the school bus or presenting the message during worship on Youth Sunday at church. These adults were taught that music demands passive listening. The youth want to combine music with doing.

For many generations devout Christians have been persuaded that the devil uses music to accomplish his evil goals. Is that the best explanation of what is happening today? Or is the new Christian music simply a normal, natural, and predictable product of the evolution from passive to active discussed earlier? Or did the rebellion of the baby boomers against their parents' values kill classical music?[12]

One response to this radical change in the context for ministry is to retire early. A second is to complain and lament the passing of the day when listeners accepted the responsibility to listen and learn. A third response is to accept the fact that television in general, and MTV in particular, has expanded the definition of effective oral communication. That expanded definition now includes: (1) the spoken word; (2) visual images; (3) music; (4) color; (5) motion; (6) frequent changes of pace; (7) humor; (8) drama; (9) emotion; (10) a perception of one-to-one communication; (11) trust; and (12) the expectation of a response from the listener-viewer.

One of the most widely known and recent examples of how to package information in a "user-friendly" style arrived on the scene in September 1982, with the founding of a new national newspaper, *USA Today.*

The first response by most journalists to this full-color newspaper with one full page of national weather reports and forecasts presented graphically in color, to the short and snappy news stories, to a relatively large number of photographs, and to an extensive and detailed sports section ranged between disdain and ridicule. This could not be serious journalism!

Fifteen years later front-page color was commonplace in metropolitan and even small-town newspapers, the two or three pages on sports had been replaced by a full sports section, news stories were shorter and faster paced, the graphics were far more attractive, and photographs were more common. In September 1997, the staid and traditionally gray *New York Times* introduced color in its daily editions.

Given the choice between serving an aging and shrinking constituency or changing, most metropolitan newspapers chose either to change or to merge into another paper.

This revolution in the definition of effective communication is of only limited significance to the congregation averaging 35, more or less, at worship that is organized around familiarity, predictability, intimacy, simplicity, caring, the perpetuating of local traditions, kinship ties, continuity with the past, and a network of one-to-one relationships with a long-tenured bivocational pastor at the hub of that network. In these congregations, effective communication is built on relationships, trust, common concerns, friendships, and a shared past.

This revolution in communication also is not a current problem in the congregation committed to ministry with adults born before 1930 who grew up and went to school in the radio era. The threat to the future of these congregations is not the electronic era, it is the mortality tables.

The very large congregations are able to afford the financial investment in the latest electronic equipment required by that worship team of five to seven staff members that includes a writer, a specialist in electronic communication, an expert in drama, one or two musicians, a couple of highly competent preachers or teachers, and a worship leader.

Currently the majority of middle-sized congregations cannot match the assets in communication of either the small congregation or the large church. That is one reason more and more midsized congregations are seeing their names on the endangered species list.

How is your congregation responding to this change in the expectations people bring to church? With optimism or despair? Either one can create a self-fulfilling prophecy!

From Survival to Choices

World War II was the most popular war in American history. A central reason for that popular support was the widely shared perception that this was a battle for survival between totalitarianism and democracy. A second reason was the clarity of the identification of a common enemy— Germany and Japan. Nearly everyone agreed that after December 7, 1941, the United States had no choice but to go to war.

A quarter of a century later, the United States was engaged in an exceptionally unpopular conflict in Vietnam. One reason for the unpopularity was the absence of a clearly identified enemy. Another was the widespread perception that the United States had had a choice on whether or not to become involved in that conflict in southeast Asia.

During the first third of the twentieth century, the majority of young men in America chose to follow in their father's footsteps in choosing a vocation. Farming; mining; teaching; the practice of law, medicine, or ministry; retail trade; and politics were among the examples of second-, third-, and fourth-generation practitioners.

Young women had fewer choices. Their list included homemaker, seamstress, nurse, teacher, clerk typist or secretary, and retail salesperson.

In the vast majority of public high schools in the 1930s, the students could choose from among sixteen to twenty-four academic courses to fulfill the state requirements for passing fifteen or sixteen academic courses in order to graduate.

The motion-picture theater on Main Street sometimes scheduled a double feature, but most of the time the choice was between seeing what was showing this week or not going to the movies.

Anyone with business at the bank took care of those transactions between nine o'clock in the morning and three in the afternoon—or waited until Saturday.

The biggest range of choices often was found in the local grocery stores, where the shelves held a dozen different types of hot and cold cereals.

In 1957 the United States Post Office issued a total of fifteen different new commemorative postage stamps.

Forty years later the U. S. Postal Service gave collectors a choice from among more than a hundred different new commemorative postage stamps.

As they prepare for adulthood, the young people of today can choose from among thousands of different occupations and vocations, many of which did not exist when their parents entered the labor force. The vast majority do not follow in their parents' footsteps.

The one-screen motion-picture theater has closed and been remodeled into a senior citizens' center or small specialized retail shops. Its successor is the sixteen- or twenty-four- or thirty-six-screen theater which offers a huge array of choices in both films and starting times.

High schools offer students a bewildering array of choices in academic subjects. Financial institutions now are open twelve to fourteen hours six days a week, and many give customers several choices as to location, including a branch in a supermarket—where two or three aisles are filled with choices in cereals.

For the first 340 years of American history, the top priority for most people was survival. After World War II, questions about identity and role moved ahead of survival goals,[13] including questions about the conduct of American foreign policy.

The generations born after World War II have been reared in a culture that has taught them that the world offers many choices and that no one can respond affirmatively to all of them.

That long list of choices includes occupation; place of residence; marital status; friendship circles; level of educational attainment; postage stamps; channels of communication with distant friends and relatives; type of motor vehicle; spouse; coffee; music; meals; parenthood; when and where to gather for the corporate worship of God; attire; hobbies; footwear; indoor temperature during the hot summer; health-care services; soft drinks; mutual funds; Internet sites; cheeses; motels; opportunities for lifetime learning; restaurants; television channels; head coverings (John F. Kennedy's lasting contribution to adult males); garden tools; religious affiliation; place of residence in retirement; pain killers; investment of discretionary financial resources; means of cross-country travel; a voice in the nomination of presidential candidates; methods of recording words and visual images for others to see, read, or hear; entertainment; academic degrees; and magazines.

Incidentally, this huge array of attractive choices available to residents of the United States and Canada is a central reason why millions of people in other parts of the world dream of the day when they will be able to emigrate to North America.

Given this huge array of choices in our culture, it should not be surprising that people who have grown up in a consumer-driven culture that is organized to expand the range of available choices expect to be offered attractive choices in the day, time, hour, physical setting, format, music, and level of expected active participation when Christians gather for the corporate worship of God. It also should not be surprising that these younger generations expect choices in the opportunities (1) to learn more about the Christian faith, (2) to be engaged in meaningful fellowship experiences with other believers, (3) to utilize their gifts, experiences, and skills in ministry with others, (4) to be challenged to do what they know they cannot do, and (5) to move to a new and higher level in their own spiritual growth.

This shift in the context for doing ministry from a culture focused on survival goals to a consumer-driven culture that overflows with choices also offers worshiping communities a range of choices. Among the most highly visible are these seven.

1. Reject this consumer-driven culture as ideologically incompatible with the Christian faith and build the future of this congregation with people born before 1930 who grew up in a world that offered most people two choices—take it or leave it.

2. Reject this demand for choices, draw the geographical area served by this congregation with a twenty- to forty-mile radius, and focus on that one-half to one percent of the population who affirm that the limited array of choices offered by this congregation represents a relevant, fulfilling, and adequate response to all the personal and religious needs of that small slice of the total population. (These are the congregations that are still constructing the 1,000- to 3,000-seat worship centers.)

3. Reject this demand for choices and be satisfied to be a

small congregation that reaches and serves the people who place intimacy, community, connections, caring, predictability, simplicity, and continuity with the past far above choices in their list of values. (This is the alternative chosen by well over one-half of all congregations in American Protestantism today and by approximately one-sixth of all churchgoers.)

4. Expand that range of attractive choices offered by this congregation as a central component of a larger strategy to reach (a) younger generations and/or (b) a broader slice of the population.

5. Define consumerism as a passing fad and plan to outlive it. Assume that the next big economic depression will recreate the value system of the 1930s, which included sacrifice, the importance of survival goals, institutional loyalties, and respect for individuals in offices of authority.

6. Redefine the role of pastor and/or program staff member from a person who does ministry to one who challenges, enlists, trains, places, nurtures, and supports teams of lay volunteers who create and staff new ministries in response to emerging new needs.

7. Rejoice in the fact that your congregation is blessed with the discretionary resources and the leadership required to offer people a choice from among three or four or five or six different worship experiences every weekend plus an exciting array of choices in learning, in discipling, in fellowship, in doing ministry, and in enriching one's own personal spiritual pilgrimage.

When the inevitable proposals are articulated to cut back on that array of choices, respond by suggesting, "Before we talk about what to eliminate or merge, let's first discuss what new ministries we should be creating to reach and serve people this congregation is not now serving. Our goal should be that before we eliminate any one of our present ministries, we should be prepared to replace it with two new ones."

Which of those seven options is the appropriate one for your congregation to consider? Which one is most consistent with the hope that the best is yet to come? Which ones are most consistent with the conviction that it is wrong to offer people so many choices?

From Enemy to Ally

When did the old-line Protestant denominations reach the peak of their strength in American Christianity and their influence in the American culture?

While they might differ on the exact year, many readers probably would agree that it was in the 1950s. Several denominations peaked in reported membership, average Sunday school attendance, and the availability of discretionary dollars in the 1950s or the early 1960s.

What is an almost guaranteed method of transforming a collection of individuals, quarreling factions, articulate dissidents, and indifferent spectators into a closely knit and unified group?

Human history suggests the most effective single organizing principle to accomplish that goal is to identify a common enemy and rally people together against that common enemy. On December 1, 1941, for example, the United States was a badly divided nation on the issue of American foreign policy. A week later, however, this was a remarkably unified country united against a couple of common enemies.

During the 1960s the Industrial Areas Foundation taught the use of this strategy as the central organizing principle for community organizers in urban America.[14] A relatively small number of Christians objected to the use of this organizing principle by the churches. Their argument was that Jesus admonished his followers to love their enemies, not to hate them. Regardless of how one responds to that debate, it is difficult to argue with the historical fact that identifying and organizing against a common enemy has been an exceptionally effective strategy for building a closely knit and cohesive following. Adolf Hitler identified the Jews as the common enemy and rallied the German people behind his goals. More recently several dictators in Africa and the Middle East have been able to rally their people around the identification of the United States as the common enemy.

Recently a young historian published a provocative essay in which he argued that from 1928 to 1960 American intellectuals rallied together against four common enemies: (1) fascism; (2) Communism; (3) racial segregation; and (4) Roman Catholicism.[15] World War II largely eliminated fascism from that list of common enemies. The 1950s found intellectuals beginning to choose up sides on the issue of Communism, but racial segregation and Roman Catholicism continued to fill the need for a common enemy.

Anti-Catholicism was a favorite rallying point for Southern Baptists, Methodists, Presbyterians, and other leaders in the mainline Protestant denominations through the 1950s. *The New Republic, The Nation,* and *The Christian Century* were among the weekly publications that fed the fires of anti-Catholicism. Seminary professors, liberal and conservative denominational leaders, and scores of respected intellectuals of the day repeatedly described the threat to American values brought by Roman Catholicism.[16]

Those readers with long memories can recall when Reformation Sunday in October was a special occasion in many Protestant congregations.

Race, which surfaced as a highly divisive issue among Baptists, Methodists, and Presbyterians in the middle of the nineteenth century, continued to be a divisive force through the 1960s.

The election of John F. Kennedy as president of the United

States; several million funerals of adults who had been reared in an anti-Catholic culture; the disappearance of Paul Blanshard as a best-selling author; the decisions made in Vatican II; the visits to North America by a pope with an attractive personality and a carefully designed public-relations program; the migration of millions of second-, third-, fourth-, and fifth-generation Roman Catholics into Protestant congregations; and the interfaith coalitions of the 1960s combined to mark the beginning of the end of an era when anti-Catholicism could be an effective organizing tool for mainstream Protestant leaders.

While it can be argued that their decisions to (a) cut back on new church development, (b) withdraw from the large central cities, (c) allocate more resources to shrinking and aging congregations, and (d) overload denominational agendas with too many top priorities were major contributing factors to the numerical decline of the mainline Protestant denominations, the loss of a common enemy undermined the internal unity of several of the larger denominations.

What can replace the common enemy as a rallying point in creating a sense of unity in a large denominational tradition? One alternative, which requires a high level of competence in the leadership, is to rally the people in support of a common goal. What has replaced opposition to fascism, to Communism, and to the Roman Catholic Church as a unifying force among Baptists, Methodists, Presbyterians, Lutherans, members of the United Church of Christ, Episcopalians, and Disciples of Christ during the last decade or two of the second millennium?

What is the common thread that unifies members of these denominations today? Is it anti-Communism? The threat of the Roman Catholic Church? Abortion? Homosexuality? The Great Commission? The role of women in the church? The future of denominationally affiliated theological schools? Planting new missions? Social justice? Evangelism? Beating the devil?[17] The Disney Company? Opposition to the use of alcoholic beverages? The threat of secret societies? Heretical teachings? Inerrancy? Doctrine? Polity? Trusting, empowering, and equipping the laity to do ministry? World missions? Raising money for pensions for aging clergy? Eliminating white racism? Advancing ecumenism? Rebuilding the inner city? American foreign policy? Maintaining control over denominational institutions (homes, hospitals, colleges, seminaries, and so forth) founded in the nineteenth century? Reform of the public welfare system? The use of smokeless tobacco by teenage boys? Promoting denominational mergers? Examining the doctrinal purity of candidates for the ministry? Collecting and redistributing money? Renaming all public schools, now attended by black children, that originally were named for a person, such as Thomas Jefferson or George Washington, who was a slaveholder?

One alternative has been chosen by several state conventions in the Southern Baptist Convention and by their new North American Mission Board. That is to make fulfillment of the Great Commission the central organizing principle. In August 1997 the Evangelical Lutheran Church in America voted to make ecumenism their central organizing principle for the next few years.

The United Methodist Church and the Presbyterian Church (U.S.A.) apparently have concluded that they enjoy sufficient internal unity and they can afford to force members to choose up sides on highly divisive issues of social justice as a top denominational agenda item.

In several denominations, various regional judicatories have chosen resourcing congregations as their primary reason for existence.

This gradual redefinition of the Roman Catholic Church in America from enemy to ally radically changed the context for ministry for both congregations and denominational systems. Instead of perceiving the Roman Catholic Church as a threat, many of today's evangelical pastors see it as a major source of future new members for their congregations!

In 1951 in his popular book *American Freedom and Catholic Power,* Paul Blanshard identifies Catholicism and Soviet Communism as the two great threats to American democracy. Forty years later the Soviet empire had collapsed, Hollywood no longer was producing the movies that romanticized the role of the Catholic priest, at least eight million adult Americans had left a Roman Catholic parish to join a Protestant congregation, the number of children enrolled in Catholic elementary parochial schools had dropped by 60 percent since 1955, and many Catholic dioceses were facing multimillion-dollar judgments from the civil courts for sexual misconduct by priests. It was increasingly difficult to build a persuasive case that Roman Catholicism was a threat to the political, social, religious, or economic components of the American culture.[18] Those changes made it easier for mainstream Protestant leaders to accept American Catholicism as a friend, an ally, and at times even a partner in ministry.

At least a few of the leaders in those religious traditions that reflect a strong western European religious culture now see the Roman Catholic Church as an ally against a new common enemy—the growing appeal of Made in America evangelicalism. That has produced a tremendous change in the context for ministry in the United States!

From Verbal to Visual

The American Bar Association in early 1997 reported that 53 percent of all large firms were using graphics as evidence or as trial exhibits in jury trials. These animations make it easier for jurors to comprehend abstract ideas or past events.

When the Federal Bureau of Investigation made its final report on the explosion of Trans World Airlines flight 800 off the coast of Long Island, they made a fifteen-minute videotape available to the national network television stations. That videotape contained a simulation of the explosion and crash and was far more persuasive than dozens of pages of printed words. No one had ever seen to this degree what that simulation revealed. Videotapes have become one of the most persuasive tools a trial lawyer can use in presenting a case to the jury. Trial lawyers operate on the premise that jurors like to be taught and the best teachers win their cases. Videotapes are persuasive teachers!

The coming of radio reinforced the Americans' dependence on oral communication in particular and on the printed and spoken word in general.

Television has revolutionized communication. More recently, the personal computer, the Internet, and the decrease in the cost of high-quality video equipment are transforming the context for ministry.

The Web site is replacing the church's ad in the Yellow Pages. The Internet is replacing the classified ads and the denominational personnel office in the search for staff. The video projector makes it possible to replace the oral illustration in the sermon with a visual one. The Internet enables the congregation to produce a parish newsletter that is updated hourly rather than mailed weekly or monthly. The mailed videotape is replacing the journey to a neutral site to hear a trial sermon by the candidate. The annual congregational report may be either on videotape or in a booklet filled with graphs, color photographs, and other visual information rather than on page after page of printed words and numbers. Television has become the most effective way to invite strangers to come to your church—and the Web site may have moved ahead of television by the time this book is published. Distance learning is raising questions about the future viability of residence-based theological education. The church library has become a resource center in which videotapes and CD-ROM disks are more numerous than books.

Pictures have replaced words as a central criterion for the creation of new generations of celebrities. Reputations of Abraham Lincoln and Franklin D. Roosevelt were and still are based largely on what each one said and did. Both are still widely quoted. The worldwide fame of Jacqueline Kennedy, Diana, the Princess of Wales, and Michael Jordan is derived largely from pictures. Rarely are their words quoted.

Another symbol of the shift from verbal to visual is the success of the newspaper *USA Today*, described earlier in this chapter.

It could be argued that the widespread ownership of the private motor vehicle, the ministry of the laity, the arrival of the electronic era, the expanding role for women in the church, the continued growth of the "enthusiastic" expression of the Christian faith, the emergence of the regional megachurch, and the decentralization of authority will stand out in the year 2050 as the seven most significant changes in the context for ministry to come out of the twentieth century.

Are those seven signs of hope or seven sources of despair? What do you think?

From Neighborhood, Church, and School to Laundromats, Bars, and the Workplace

One of the reasons parents encouraged their sons and daughters to enroll in a denominationally affiliated college in the first half of the twentieth century was to meet a compatible future spouse. Lutheran boys met and married Lutheran girls, as did Baptists, Jews, Methodists, Roman Catholics, Presbyterians, and others.

Likewise northerners married northerners, southerners

married southerners, persons from an Italian ancestry married Italians, blacks married blacks, Native Americans married Native Americans, Scandinavians married Scandinavians, Germans married Germans, Japanese married Japanese, rural residents married rural residents, and urbanites married urbanites. People also tended to marry within their social class when they chose a spouse.

As recently as 1960 the median age for the first marriage for men was 22.8 years and 20.3 years for women. By 1990 those two numbers had climbed to 25.9 years and 24.0 years respectively.

For most of American history people first met their future spouse from among the residents of their neighborhood or in church or in school.

That remarkable migration from rural America to the cities that began in the 1920s and 1930s and exploded after World War II began to change that tradition.

A common pattern was for the wedding ceremony to be scheduled a few days after graduation from the college or university. This enabled the parents to combine two celebrations into one trip, made it easier to select graduation presents, and also was a convenient time for friends and classmates to attend.

During the third quarter of the twentieth century, bars, laundromats, night-school classes, bicycle trips, and parties emerged as places to meet a potential future spouse.

More recently, partly as a result of that sharp increase in remarriages, partly as a result of the postponement of marriage to later in life, and partly as a result in the increased numbers of women in the labor force, the workplace has become a popular place to meet one's future spouse.

Today the sons of Korean immigrants marry women of European ancestry. Blacks marry Anglos. Catholics marry Protestants. National ancestry is far less of a factor in choosing a spouse than it was two or three generations ago.

Southerners marry northerners. Farm girls marry men who have never been within forty feet of a cow, combine, or manure spreader. Between one-third and one-half of all Jews marry someone from outside that religious tradition. Baptists marry Episcopalians, Asians marry Anglos, and Latinos marry Koreans to produce a trilingual family.

Perhaps the least widely discussed of all these points of discontinuity with the recent past concerns the consequences of the marriage of a Catholic and Protestant or a Lutheran and a Baptist. In the 1950s the usual result was that newly married couples ended up in the church with which one of them had exceptionally strong ties. Three out of four couples in 1955, for example, in a Catholic-Protestant marriage became members of a Catholic parish. Today that proportion is one out of four.

Today couples coming from two different religious traditions frequently decide, "We won't join your church and we won't join my church; we'll pick a religious tradition new to both of us." For many the most attractive compromise is the nondenominational or independent congregation.

One result is that two of the reliable entry points for new members of the 1950s—being born into that denomination and/or congregation and marrying into that church—have shrunk dramatically in significance. For many, marriage is a point of entry for newcomers; for many others, marriage is a point of departure.

In the 1960s and the 1970s, the singles ministry provided an opportunity for the person in his or her midtwenties to meet a potential future spouse who shared the same value system and religious orientation. By the late 1980s, however, a growing proportion of the participants in these ministries were older, formerly married adults. That group was no longer an attractive hunting ground for the never-married twenty-seven-year-old.

One substitute was the laundromat. Another was the bar.

A third was a cruise. A fourth was the beach or swimming pool. A fifth was the condominium occupied largely by single adults.

The most popular place to meet that future spouse, however, has turned out to be the place of work.

More recently, several congregations have designed new vocal groups, teams of volunteers to construct a Habitat for Humanity house, self-improvement groups, recreation ministries, bicycle trips, Bible study groups, mission-work camp trips, Saturday evening dinners followed by worship and study, community-service ministries, worship teams, tutoring programs, and night classes with three goals in mind: (1) to meet a need; (2) to provide an attractive entry point for potential future members; and (3) to create opportunities for single adults born after 1965 to meet a potential future spouse.

What if it works? One consequence is a new question for congregational self-appraisal. How many marriages did we help to make happen?

A second and far more complicated one concerns baptism. As we bring into our congregation people who come from a different tradition than ours regarding baptism, how do we respond to that issue? Do we require one or both to be rebaptized? Or do we accept the validity of their baptism? Or do we create a category of "associate member," which means a second-class role?

One response is to accept this as a fact of contemporary reality and an explanation for shrinking numbers. An alternative is to design and offer ministries that provide opportunities for adults born after 1965 to meet that future spouse. Many people, especially never-married men, are eager to find a potential spouse who is a committed Christian, who places a high value on a traditional system of moral values, and who also is looking for a future spouse. They view the church as the best place to conduct that search. Can your church help them?

From Too Young to Too Late

In April 1988, Ewing Marion Kauffman promised the 247 eighth-grade students at Westport Middle School in Kansas City that he would pay for four years of college if they would stay off drugs, graduate from high school on schedule, avoid parenthood, and earn good grades. During the next nine years, the Kauffman Foundation spent over $22 million on 1,394 disadvantaged youth to fulfill that promise.

Several critics of Mr. Kauffman's generosity contended that this effort at intervention came too early. Those dollars could have been spent more productively by offering scholarships to high school seniors to enable them to go on to college.

Head Start was an innovative program launched by the federal government in the early 1960s. It was based on the assumption that the early years of formal schooling should not be postponed until the five-year-old child was old enough to go to kindergarten. Tens of thousands of children, ages three and four, could benefit from a head start in their schooling. Families who did not qualify for Head Start agreed and began the search for the nursery school where they could enroll their three-year-old and four-year-old children. Many Head Start programs and nursery schools were housed in church buildings. Many parents and grandparents, however, objected. They argued that the formal schooling process should not begin before age five. Three-year-olds clearly were too young to be out of the home and in that environment for that long period of time.

Today, thanks to the research conducted during the 1990s by dozens of neuroscientists, we know that the first two or three years of life are crucial in how the brain "hardwires" itself.[19] One result is a rapid increase in the number of congregations with a highly skilled staff, both paid and volunteer, who help parents learn how to appropriately intellectually stimulate their baby during the first months of life. Three years is not too early for a child to be in nursery school, and age three is too late to begin an effective process for the healthy intellectual, emotional, moral, and social development of a child.

This shift from intervening at the age many thought was too early, and is now seen as too late, has had a profound impact on the context for ministry. This can be illustrated by several questions.

Do you agree our culture is an increasingly barren and hostile environment for children? Would you like to see every baby given the opportunity to blossom into the person God intended that child to become? Do you agree that the process of procreation does not automatically endow the parents with the knowledge and skills required to be effective and nurturing parents? Would you like to see that congregation with an aging and shrinking membership grow younger and larger? Do you agree that more than intuition is required to be a good parent today? Do you believe the Christian churches could and should be the pioneer in making this a better environment for children?

If you respond affirmatively to all six questions, you may agree with this observer that potentially the most significant change in the secular context for ministry during the past few decades can be summarized in one brief sentence. We know far more than we did twenty years ago about how to nurture the healthy emotional, intellectual, and social development of very young children.

The three missing components are (1) a commitment to utilize that research to help parents become more effective mothers and fathers, (2) a delivery system to make that happen, and (3) the institutional infrastructure to generate commitment and to support the delivery system.

Today's churches are at a fork in the road. One alternative is to watch passively as public and private schools and other secular institutions design and build the needed delivery systems. This was the alternative chosen by most churches as they learned more about how to help alcoholics, to respond to the needs of parents who had experienced the death of a child, or to minister to new generations of teenagers and college students. Alcoholics Anonymous, Compassionate Friends, and a variety of parachurch organizations were created in response to those needs.

The second alternative is for congregations and denominational systems to accept the pioneering role of creating those new delivery systems. The urgent need is for a system that will intervene during that critical four-year window of opportunity—from before conception to the child's third birthday.

Will your church be one of the pioneers in building that delivery system?

This central theme of beginning early rather than waiting until it may be too late can be illustrated by another set of questions.

1. When should a child be exposed to several hours of music every day? Long before the child's first birthday.

2. If the goal is to produce a happy, healthy, and enduring marriage, when should intervention begin? Ideally in the very early years of life, when that child is reared by a couple in a happy and healthy marriage.

3. At what age should theological schools begin to enlist future students? Probably while they are in middle school.

4. When will the decision be made as to whether a Christian congregation will be a high expectation church or a low expectation parish? In the criteria used to select the minister responsible for creating that new mission.

5. When should congregations invite parents to enroll in their first parent-training class? Ideally at least three or four or five months before the birth of their first child.

6. At what age should a church begin a systematic stew-

ardship-education program? No later than when a child first begins to receive a weekly allowance.

7. When should a child begin to take lessons on a musical keyboard? Well before that child's third birthday.

8. When is the best time to help people acquire the skills required to meet and make new friends and to nurture meaningful friendship ties? Long before ninth grade.

9. When should a new mission schedule its first public worship service? In three out of four new missions, not until after an extensive ministry with parents of young children has been designed and staffed and is being implemented.

10. When does a person's mental capability to learn and integrate new information begin to plateau? At about age three.

11. When should the church nursery be transformed from a custodial function into a stimulating learning environment? Well before the first baby arrives to be cared for in that nursery.

12. When does a person begin to appreciate learning from the printed word? During the first year of life.

These questions help to explain why it is more difficult to be an effective parish pastor today than it was forty years ago. They also introduce the subject of what has become known as the therapeutic society.

From Sympathy to Intervention

How do Americans respond to the plight of the poor, the widowed, the unemployed, the unmarried mother, the alcoholic, the orphan, the homeless, the mentally incompetent, the hungry, the person with physical disabilities, and the troubled?

One response has been sympathy. A second has been an admonition to be more self-reliant. A third has been to urge people to accept the present consequences of earlier actions. A fourth has been to construct and financially subsidize a variety of institutions such as orphanages, hospitals, shelters, food kitchens, homes, and schools. A fifth has been to create other forms of intervention.

The nineteenth century in America brought the introduction of a variety of forms of intervention by both public and private agencies to improve the lives of the poor, the widows, the orphans, and others who lived on the margins of society.

The nineteenth century also saw the churches mobilize the resources required to build and operate hospitals, orphanages, homes for elderly widows, and a variety of other institutions.

The twentieth century brought a demand for publicly funded pensions and allowances as well as an expansion of the social services available to the lower class.[20] What is sometimes referred to as the "therapeutic state"[21] continued to expand during the past several decades and now includes assistance for middle- and upper-income citizens in the form of entitlements, counseling, and public services. The elderly now outnumber the poor as the recipients of financial help and services.

One evidence of the recent growth of the therapeutic society is in employment. According to the U. S. Bureau of Labor Statistics, between 1960 and 1990 the population of the United States increased by 40 percent, the number of farmers decreased by 50 percent, the number of lawyers increased by 260 percent, the number of clergypersons grew by 67 percent, the number of elementary school teachers rose by 35 percent, and the number of counselors of various types increased by 1,700 percent!

By far the most significant consequence in denominational circles of the emergence of the therapeutic society has been the change in the frame of reference and in the language. An increasing array of divisive issues, ranging from world missions to abortion to ethnic separation to gender to evangelism to ministries with teenagers to the pedagogical approach of theological schools, are being discussed in therapeutic language rather than in New Testament language. Scripture, doctrine, and tradition provide the frame of reference and the language for one side in these discussions, while the other side approaches the issue with a therapeutic frame of reference and language.

If one side presented their arguments in Russian and the other in Portuguese, that would make it easier to recognize (a) the existence of a problem in communication and (b) why the general public tends to ignore the whole debate.

The tendency for many congregations to become bilingual as some leaders rely on the therapeutic language while others prefer the New Testament language is one more reason why it is more difficult to be a parish pastor today than it was in the 1950s.

Among the other consequences for the practice of ministry are these: (1) the introduction of the sermon in the 1950s that was organized around a pastoral-counseling theme; (2) the expectation that every pastor would be a competent and helpful pastoral counselor (a trend that apparently peaked in the 1980s); (3) the creation of new therapeutic models for ministries with teenagers; (4) the creation of a huge variety of self-help and "twelve-step" ministries by congregations as a group response to the demand for help; (5) the increasing number of people enrolling in theological seminaries who perceive the seminary to be either (a) a therapy center and/or (b) a place to help one advance to the next stage in one's personal spiritual pilgrimage; (6) the establishment of pastoral-counseling centers in churches in the 1970s and 1980s and the cosponsorship of off-campus counseling centers in the late 1980s and the 1990s; (7) the expectations by the federal government in the 1990s that both congregations and denominational systems will become active partners with governmental agencies in a sharp expansion of the therapeutic society; (8) the creation of professional staff positions in congregations, many funded by governmental agencies or hospitals or foundations or corporations, to provide specialized helping services to those in need; (9) an increase in the number of seminary graduates who choose employment in the human-services sector of the labor force over the parish ministry as a vocation; (10) the incorporation of single-function nonprofit 501(c)3 corporations by congregations (this is more common among African American congregations than among Anglo churches); (11) the emergence of local interfaith coalitions to respond to a variety of needs from feeding the hungry to sheltering the homeless to helping adults move from welfare to work; and (12) the growing number of congregations that derive at least one half of their total receipts (rents, fees, grants, tuition, or designated gifts) from some form of participation in the delivery of human services.

One consequence is that more and more congregational leaders are asking, "Are we primarily in the religion business or primarily in the social-welfare business?"

Another consequence is that more and more congregations are being invited to enter into partnerships with governmental agencies, corporations, private welfare organizations, foundations, universities, hospitals, and other philanthropic and charitable groups to respond to the human needs identified by the therapeutic society.

How has your congregation been affected by the rise of the therapeutic society? What is the preferred language of your new volunteer leaders? Is it the same as your veteran leaders? Do you, as a pastor, use the same language as your predecessor?

From Talk Therapy to Drugs to the Internet

A growing body of medical research indicates that drug therapy may be more effective in treating certain psychological disorders than counseling. This has encouraged many insurance companies and health maintenance organizations to place a fairly low ceiling on reimbursements for the cost of counseling services.

These two trends have coincided with that tremendous increase in (a) the number of persons who are willing to talk with a stranger about their personal problems; (b) the number of parishioners who believe that counseling, along with worship, fellowship, and learning, is among the services that churches should offer people; and (c) the number of persons with a master's degree or a doctorate in psychology, pastoral counseling, or some other form of talk therapy.

The 1960s and the 1970s brought a remarkable increase in the number of parish pastors who explained that they devoted fifteen to thirty hours a week in counseling individuals or couples. The 1980s brought the recognition that the counselor was severely limited in attempting to work with a troubled sixteen-year-old in a series of one-to-one sessions. A more productive approach was to work with that whole family constellation.

The early 1990s brought a new frame of reference. Since few ministers are licensed to prescribe drugs, it would be a better stewardship of time for that pastor to concentrate on mastering how to make the appropriate referrals.

This increasing emphasis on drug therapy also has affected the role of (a) the professional counseling center created and supported by several congregations, (b) the theological schools that offer a master's degree or a doctorate in pastoral counseling, and (c) the thousands of individual counselors in private practice who are not licensed to prescribe drugs.

The 1990s also brought a growing concern about the number of pastors who engaged in inappropriate sexual behavior with female parishioners. One clinical psychologist describes this as "a deal struck between greed and need."

One result is the change from males counseling females to females counseling females.[22]

The late 1990s brought a new player to the therapeutic society. This is the Internet. The Internet now provides (a) a growing variety of faceless therapy and mutual support groups; (b) the opportunity to interact with someone who was experiencing exactly the same problem a year or two earlier; (c) a place for public scrutiny of obituaries, eulogies, and memorial services; (d) Web pages to serve as memorials for the deceased; and (e) virtual cemeteries. By 2005 the number of people who come to the church for the memorial service may be a tiny fraction of those who watch it via the Internet or on their home television screen. The old assumption was the longer you lived, the smaller the crowd at your funeral. The new assumption is the longer you live, the more people the Internet will enable to watch your memorial service.

Today any congregation with access to the Internet can create a national or international group-therapy ministry, staffed by professionals or by trained laypeople or by completely incompetent volunteers, to counsel people who have problems but are afraid of drugs and are too shy to engage in a one-to-one counseling effort.

These are a few of the reasons that several veteran pastors contend the greatest point of discontinuity with the past in the parish ministry is in how we intervene in people's lives.

What do you think? Is this a sign of hope? Or a cause for alarm?

4
SEVEN NEGLECTED CHANGES

Which of these many points of discontinuity with the past is the number one sign of hope for the churches in the twenty-first century? If pressed, this observer's initial response would be, "Let's wait and see." A second response would be the combined impact of the Fourth Great Awakening and the expanded role of the laity.

A different question evokes a different response. What are the most widely neglected points of discontinuity with the past? That question leads to cutting down a few more trees for another chapter.

From Service to Challenge

A widely shared assumption of the 1950s, although rarely stated this simply, was that congregations existed (1) to gather people together for the corporate worship of God, for the proclamation of the Word, and for the administration of the sacraments or ordinances; (2) to take care of the personal and spiritual needs of the members and their children; (3) to maintain the real estate; and (4) in one way or another, to convert nonbelievers into believers. A large share of the budget often was allocated to the first and third of those four responsibilities.

In simple terms, the minister and the congregation were

expected to respond to the personal and spiritual needs of the members. It was not unusual to hear a pastor reflect, "During my first four years in the ministry, I served a small rural congregation. After that, I served as the pastor of a church in a county-seat town, and six years ago I came here to serve this suburban congregation." The role of the minister was to serve the people.

In recent years a growing number of pastors, most of whom were born in 1952 or later, have redefined their primary role.

One facet of this new definition of their role is to encourage believers to become learners, to challenge learners to become fully devoted disciples of Jesus Christ, and to equip disciples to become volunteers in ministry. One consequence is that many of these pastors use the term "teacher" or "speaker" rather than "preacher" to describe their speaking role.

An overlapping definition is offered by those pastors who define the role of the worshiping community as a transformational environment where people's lives are changed. The obvious implication is that if the central goal of that congregation is the transformation of people's lives, values, behavior, attitudes, and belief systems, success will automatically produce great discontinuity with the past in both the people as individuals and in that institutional expression of the Christian faith.

Among the many consequences of this redefinition of the role of the pastor are these six.

1. The new minister who is effective in designing and implementing a strategy built around challenge and transformation and who follows a long-tenured pastor who affirmed the role of "serve the people" probably will (a) need a high level of competence in conflict resolution, (b) have to bid farewell to a few dozen longtime members

who prefer a congregation designed to serve the people, and (c) find it necessary to enlist a new cadre of volunteer leaders and policymakers.

2. This line of demarcation between the congregation organized to serve the members and the one designed to challenge people is a far more significant factor in identity than the denominational affiliation or the personal characteristics of the members or the location of the meeting place.

3. The assignment to create a new congregation organized around challenging people is far easier to carry out than the call to transform a long-established congregation organized around serving the current membership into one that transforms believers into disciples.

Thus the denomination committed to increasing the number of high expectation congregations will place a relatively high priority on starting new missions and a low priority on transforming long-established low expectation congregations into high expectation churches.

4. This distinction is becoming an increasingly significant line of demarcation in classifying theological schools. One group prepares students to go out to serve congregations. Another group prepares students around the twin themes of challenge and transformation.

5. A small but growing number of pastors have concluded that, if their central goal is to persuade nonbelievers of the truth and relevance of the gospel of Jesus Christ, the first step must be the transformation of the current members who are believers into disciples and apostles.

6. The easiest way to avoid this issue is to encourage short pastorates of two to four years.

From Toys to Experiences

A bumper sticker of the 1980s declared, "The one who dies with the most toys wins the game." This reflected a simplistic disdain for a consumer-driven society. The pendulum had swung from an era of scarcity in the 1930s and 1940s to an era of affluence. In the 1930s a telephone in the home was a luxury; in the 1960s a telephone in the home was a necessity. By the 1980s two or three telephones in the home had moved from a luxury to a convenience. By the late 1990s necessity required three or four telephones in the home, plus one in the car, one in the briefcase, one in the purse, and one in the bag a teenager carried to high school and on to work.

The increase in the number of privately owned motor vehicles, bathrooms, television sets, summer cottages, electronic devices, bedrooms, and computer terminals reflected this desire to collect lots of toys before death arrived.

In ecclesiastical circles the drive to collect more toys was reflected in new church development; in the expansion of the paid program staff; and in an increase in academic degrees, awards, radio broadcasts, videotapes, books, church members, and building programs.

And then came a new generation. Instead of searching for more collectibles, as had their parents and grandparents, many of this new generation concentrated on collecting experiences.[1]

What do people collect? The experience of a bicycle trip through southern France. The experience of sleeping in the Lincoln bedroom in the White House. Listening to a creative individual read his or her poetry. Giving birth to a baby without any anesthetic. Climbing a very high mountain. Going on a 450-mile bike ride with a thousand others to raise money for a worthy cause. Attending the funeral service of a famous person. Shaking hands with the president of the United States. Skateboarding. Taking a cruise through the Panama Canal. Spending ten days in the Holy Land. Mastering a challenging computer game in the arcade. Taking a train ride through the Rockies. Auditing a class taught by a Nobel Prize winner. Finishing the 26.2-mile

Boston Marathon. Enjoying the thrilling rides at an amusement park. Attending a Catholic mass celebrated by the pope. Shopping at the Mall of America in suburban Minneapolis. Dining in the Rainforest Cafe or some similar restaurant. Learning to fly an airplane. Worshiping at Willow Creek Community Church or some other famous megachurch.

Like the change in the national dress code that began in the 1960s, this switch from collecting toys to collecting experiences is (a) contagious and (b) caught by older people from younger people.

Perhaps the most interesting consequence of this shift from collecting things to collecting experiences is the growing number of tourists who design their trip so they can visit one of the famous African American or black churches in New York or Chicago or San Francisco on Sunday morning or worship with one of the better-known white megachurches.

Far more important, however, is the reconceptualization of the corporate worship of God from a "service" to an "experience." One facet of this is the new Christian music. Bob Dylan declared he found "religiosity and philosophy in the music. . . . The songs are my lexicon. I believe the songs."

The most significant aspect of this discontinuity is the growth of the charismatic renewal movement, especially among upper-middle- and upper-class Anglos. A central part of that movement is to experience the baptism of the Holy Spirit. Other aspects of this discontinuity include the phenomenon of the Promise Keepers rallies in the mid-1990s, the 1997 "Stand in the Gap" rally in Washington, and the spread of a new version of evangelistic rallies.

Another consequence of this shift to collecting experiences can be seen in several new models for youth ministries. The old formula of food, fun, fellowship, and study has stiff competition. One is the national youth rally with thousands of teenage participants. A second is the mission-work trip experience. A third is the youth choir trip to Europe. A fourth is the two- to ten-month youth exchange program with a church on another continent. A fifth is the overnight lock-in. A sixth is the rally around the flagpole at school.

Finally, this is changing the learning experiences offered by congregations. Instead of devoting thirteen weeks to a study of the Reformation, that adult Sunday school class spends ten days walking in Martin Luther's footsteps in Europe. Instead of bringing a seminary professor to lecture on John Wesley, that class goes to England for a week. Instead of studying a book on church renewal, the leaders of that congregation spend three days in a workshop offered by teaching church A. Three months later they attend a workshop offered by teaching church B, and a few months later they visit teaching church C.

The basic generalization is that the younger the adults in the congregation and/or the newer they are to the Christian faith, the greater the emphasis on an experiential approach to the faith.

From Belief to Unbelief

Of all the changes that have occurred in the cultural or secular context for ministry in the United States, the most challenging is summarized in the subtitle of a book published in the mid-1980s.[2] In this volume, history professor James Turner argues that for at least a thousand years, western Europeans—and for nearly three centuries, Americans of European ancestry—had assumed the existence of God. The details and the doctrinal positions might vary, but the existence of God as the Creator was a given that was beyond challenge. By 1790, millennial expectations had emerged as a line of demarcation, but neither side challenged the existence of God.

Turner identifies the 1850–70 era as the time when "the

intellectual ground of belief in God" was transformed from bedrock into gelatin.[3] The term *agnosticism* was invented by Thomas Huxley in 1869.[4] That word identified a legitimate position between belief and unbelief that became increasingly popular.

A list of famous men who helped advance the acceptance of unbelief would include René Descartes, Thomas Hobbes, Voltaire, David Hume, Dennis Diderot, Friedrich Nietzsche, Karl Marx, Sigmund Freud, Jeremy Bentham, Thomas Huxley, Bertrand Russell, Mark Twain, Henry L. Mencken, and John Dewey.

By 1902 William James had identified the beauty and power of nature as a religious successor to Christianity. Unbelief had become a "fully available" option. Advocacy of traditional moral principles became an alternative to a belief in God.

One of the interesting points Turner makes is that most of the highly articulate proponents of unbelief in the last third of the nineteenth century came out of a very broadly defined Reformed western European religious tradition. Many were among the leading intellectuals of their day, and a fair number were clergymen who had moved from belief to unbelief. Institutions of higher education were among the most effective in advocating that belief in God was a matter of personal choice, not a given for understanding the world in which we live.[5]

In recent years this shift from belief in God to an acceptance of unbelief has been diluted by another trend. This is sometimes described as "faith in faith," rather than faith in a God alive and at work in the world. This trend has been nurtured by a recent wave of nonsectarian religious television programs and by scores of novels and nonfiction books that focus on spirituality and a person's spiritual journey but with little or no reference to a Trinitarian expression of the Christian gospel.

From this observer's perspective, it appears that the societal acceptance of unbelief as a legitimate option surfaced first in America among intellectuals. Later it became an acceptable option for middle- and working-class Americans. Only recently has unbelief begun to become a legitimate option for American-born blacks—and many will argue that that is one of the most significant lines of demarcation between American-born Anglos and African Americans. This line of demarcation stands out most clearly when the theologically very liberal white congregation seeks to reach and serve American-born blacks.

The acceptance of unbelief as a legitimate option for every citizen and that new wave of "faith in faith" have radically transformed the context for pastoral ministry from what it was in 1750 or 1850 or even 1950! That is one reason why it is more difficult to be an effective and happy parish pastor today than it was forty or sixty years ago.

From the Center to the Margins

What were the differences in the daily schedules of the student attending a church-related college in Michigan in 1859 and the student attending a non-church-related college in Michigan that same year?

One difference was that the student in the Christian college attended chapel twice a day, while chapel attendance was required only once a day at the nonsectarian state university.[6]

One of the most frequently expressed regrets by Christian leaders in the United States concerns the erosion of the influence of traditional Christian moral values and standards of behavior. Through the 1930s, and in many communities well into the 1960s and 1970s, the public schools resembled tax-supported evangelical Protestant institutions. State legislatures and city councils adopted legislation that limited commercial activity on Sunday morning. In many school districts Wednesday evening was "church night," and the public schools were careful not to schedule competing activities for that evening.

No one can dispute that the influence of Christianity in the public schools in the United States is far less today than it was in the first half of the twentieth century.

It could be argued that the one slice of society in which the Christian faith has most clearly moved from the center to the margins is in higher education.

For most of the years since western Europeans emigrated to North America, higher education was the creation of the Christian churches. Harvard University, the oldest institution of higher education in the United States, was founded in 1636 and named for a Puritan clergyman. For more than seven decades at least one-half of Harvard graduates entered the ministry. For more than two hundred years, most of the institutions of higher education in the United States were avowedly Christian schools.

When William Rainey Harper agreed to become the founding president of the University of Chicago, he insisted that the Divinity School be at the center of the university. It was assumed that the Christian faith would permeate and undergird the teachings of all the other schools and departments in the university.[7]

As recently as the 1930s, many of the megachurches of that day, the Protestant congregations averaging a thousand or more at worship, were university churches.

By the mid-1950s it was widely assumed, and in several traditions it was a legal requirement, that a seminary degree was an essential credential for ordination as a parish pastor. That also was the day when many denominational leaders came out in support of the goal that a theological school should be "urban, ecumenical, and university-related." Those are fragments from one side of the picture. The twentieth century revealed another side of the picture.

By 1950 it was increasingly unrealistic to expect that theological schools could and would (a) transmit the doctrines and teachings of the orthodox Christian faith and (b) affirm and transmit denominational traditions to new generations of students.[8] The gap between Jerusalem, the city of faith, and Athens, the city of knowledge, continued to widen. A growing number of university scholars began to describe "Christian scholarship" as an oxymoron.[9] When senior pastors of megachurches are asked how that nearby theological school could resource their congregation or undergird their ministry, the most frequently articulated response is the equivalent of "Beats me."

When Andrew Carnegie offered in 1906 to fund a pension system for university and college teachers, it was designed to reduce the number of denominationally affiliated schools. That was accomplished by limiting participation by private schools to those that did not carry a denominational affiliation. At that time, there were only 51 nondenominational private schools compared to 218 with a denominational tie.[10] Shortly after that, scores of schools became "nonsectarian" in order to participate in the Carnegie pension fund.

The competition for students and private gifts of the post-1970 era motivated dozens of other church-related colleges and universities to sever or minimize their denominational ties.

The road to fame for a university today is not from the Christian commitment of the faculty nor the huge crowds that gather every Sunday morning at the university church but rather from (a) the national rankings of its basketball or football teams, (b) the research grants awarded to the faculty, and (c) the rankings of the school's academic quality published by a variety of sources, including both faculty and students. Frequently parachurch organizations have a greater impact on the spiritual pilgrimage of the students than does the denominational identity of the school. In those universities that include a divinity school, these parachurch organizations may reach a larger number of undergraduates than does the divinity school housed on that campus.

It is almost certain that the long-term effects of the marginalization of the Christian faith in higher education in the United States have yet to be felt. That could turn out to be an exceptionally influential change in the context for ministry in the twenty-first century.

One of the consequences is already well underway. That is to relocate the preparation of future generations of parish pastors from the campus of the theological school to the campus of the teaching church. Like other radical changes, it will be (a) resisted by those with a powerful attachment to the status quo, (b) opposed by the guardians of the present capital investment, and (c) fully implemented only after several hundred crucial funerals have been held. These funerals will not be scheduled, however, until after the investment of tens of millions of additional dollars in the construction of new buildings, both classrooms and residential facilities, and the renovation of the old structures on the campuses of scores of existing theological schools. Well-endowed institutions rarely die, they simply invest more money in redefining their role.

A second consequence is that fewer and fewer Christians expect that the colleges and universities founded to transmit the orthodox Christian faith and denominational doctrine and traditions to future generations will be able to accomplish that with the students of the twenty-first century.

A third, and perhaps the most important, consequence is the emergence of a new line of demarcation in classifying institutions of higher education in the twenty-first century. To use Professor James Turner's system, which institutions will be perceived as nurturing belief and which will be perceived as fostering unbelief?

From Unifying to Divisive

A persuasive argument can be made that the single most unifying episode in American history was the shared experiences of the Mormons who made the journey from Nauvoo, Illinois, to Salt Lake City under the leadership of Brigham Young in 1846–47.[11] That long, dangerous, and difficult shared experience had a powerful unifying impact on the survivors.

A second example of a unifying shared experience that produced a lifelong cohesive impact in a generation of survivors was shared by those who fought in the Confederate armies in the Civil War.

More recently the survivors of the Great Depression of 1929–37 frequently referred to that unifying experience for another three or four decades. World War II filled that need for an even greater number of Americans through the 1980s.

"Where were you when Pearl Harbor was attacked?" eventually was replaced by, "Do you remember where you were when you heard that President Kennedy had been shot?"

For many Americans born in the 1910–28 era, the experiences and memories of the Great Depression and World War II provided them with a shared and unifying national experience that shaped their identity forever.

To a lesser extent the age cohorts born in the 1929–42, 1943–55, and 1956–68 periods shared several defining experiences that made it possible to describe in positive terms each of those age cohorts as a generation. Perhaps the number one example consists of American women born in the 1930s, who were more likely to marry, to marry early in life, to become mothers, and to pioneer new opportunities in the labor force than any other age cohort of American-born women. It is possible to identify several common characteristics shared by a large proportion of Americans born in the post-1968 era, but that age cohort did not share in a unifying national experience that defined their identity as a generation. This generation of American people did not experience a memorable and widely shared event comparable to the Civil War, the Great Depression, World War II, the Civil Rights movement, or the conflict in Vietnam. The closest to that was the explosion of the space vehicle, *Challenger*, in January 1986.[12]

From 1945 through 1985, generational theory was a useful paradigm for designing marketing strategies for automobile manufacturers, clothing designers, religious congregations, colleges, magazines, and restaurants, but recent years have brought challengers. Today the marketing experts focus on narrowly defined subgroups within each age cohort. Perhaps the number one example of this in the churches is the inability to find one expression of Christian music that is meaningful or even acceptable to the generation born in the 1956–68 period. The churches that are most effective in reaching members of the largest age cohort in American history usually offer two or three different worship experiences every weekend, each with its own distinctive type of music.

Likewise, no one has devised a single strategy that will enable a congregation to reach and serve a majority of today's high school students.

Perhaps the best evidence of the absence of a widely shared defining national experience for Americans born after 1968 or 1969 is the variety of birth years used by today's proponents of generational theory to describe the younger age cohorts in the American population.

Life was simpler and easier when we could speak with great confidence about the common characteristics of the 1910–28 generation or the women born in the 1930s or "the front edge of the baby boomers."

For fifty years generational theory provided a unifying

thread in defining potential constituencies for a congregation's ministry. Today that conceptual framework often leads to highly divisive discussions about what to do and how to do it.

A second example of the shift from unifying to divisive can be seen in the agendas of many denominational systems. (This is discussed in more detail in the section "A Denominational Perspective" in the next chapter.) In the 1950s the agenda of the national convention for that denomination or the annual meeting of the regional judicatory typically included several unifying reports and challenges and only two or three divisive issues. Today that agenda may call for allocating large quantities of time to several controversial and divisive issues and a comparatively modest amount of time to celebrating victories and lifting up unifying themes.

These are simply two more in that long list of reasons to explain why being a parish pastor today is far more difficult than it was in the 1950s.

From Higher to Wider

A combination of five factors has sharply increased the cost of providing adequate physical facilities for a Christian congregation. One, discussed in the second chapter, is the replacement of the neighborhood congregation, with a walk-in constituency, by the large regional church. The second is that two or three or four times as many motor vehicles are required today, as compared to the 1950s, to bring one hundred people to church.

A third is that while per capita personal income in the United States increased approximately seventeenfold between 1950 and 1998, the cost of land for religious uses increased thirty to two hundred times. The three-acre parcel of farmland out on the far edge of the city that sold for $2,000 to $3,500 in 1950 cost $60,000 to $600,000 in 1998.

A fourth factor is that the churchgoers of today bring far greater expectations to church than was the pattern in the 1950s. Many not only expect a vacant and conveniently located parking space, they also expect a first-floor nursery for babies, another room for toddlers, and a playroom for children ages sixteen months to twenty-four months; a large narthex or "milling around" space next to the room designed for worship; a single-purpose choir rehearsal room with risers; three or four times as many restrooms as the norm for the 1950s; a variety of comfortable meeting rooms; a gymnasium; a fellowship hall; an attractive office area for staff; an air-conditioned building; an outdoor playground for young children; a soccer field; a volleyball court; and possibly, a softball diamond plus a picnic area. The indoor running track is increasingly common, but the indoor swimming pool probably is a generation or two into the future for most congregations.

The fifth point of discontinuity with the past is the primary symbol for identification. As recently as the 1950s, "a tall steeple church" was a synonym for the congregation that included a disproportionately large number of the "movers and shakers" from among the community leaders. The Methodist congregation designing a new building often made sure its steeple would reach farther into the sky than the steeple on the Episcopal or Presbyterian or Roman Catholic building. A few years later the new Baptist church had the tallest steeple in town. Church steeples often were the tallest structures in town.

The height of the steeple no longer is an influential bragging point. One successor is the size of the parking lot. Even better, however, is the fact that everything is on one floor. The basement disappeared from construction in the 1980s. Wherever possible, the stairway to the second floor was eliminated. It disappeared a few years after those big one-story retail boxes across the street from the two- or three-story shopping mall began to draw shoppers away from the mall.

One consequence is that the ten- to twenty-acre church site has become the norm. The exceptions are not the five- to seven-acre sites of the 1960s and 1970s. The highly visible exceptions for the twenty-first century are the forty- to two-hundred-acre relocation sites being acquired by congregations founded before 1970 and the sites being purchased by the new congregations that reflect a Made in America religious identity.

One of the consequences of this is the growing opposition of officials in local government who object to that much land being removed from the tax roll.

Another is the policy question confronting those concerned with new church development. Should we plan to launch ten new missions, each on a five- to ten-acre site? Or should we invest our limited resources in purchasing a sixty- to two-hundred-acre site for what will be a regional megachurch?

Paralleling that is the question before the leaders of that aging congregation that meets in a three-story building constructed before 1960 on a site covering 15,000 square feet of land. "Should we invest our money in remodeling this obsolete structure on this inadequate site or should we relocate to a larger parcel of land and construct a new one-story building?"

From One Site to Many

"That's the First National Bank at the corner of Main and Washington, and directly across from it is First Church, where we've been members ever since we moved here thirty years ago. The college is four blocks to the east up on the hill, our hospital is about a half mile to the west, and our doctor has his office in that building over there," explained the longtime resident in 1965 while showing an old friend around town.

Today's resident takes a visiting friend on a brief visit to the same part of town and explains, "That's the First National Bank, but I haven't been there for years. We do all our banking at a branch in the supermarket where we buy groceries. We're members of First Church, but we go to their east-side campus, which is within walking distance of our house. We have one congregation, one staff, one budget, and one treasury, but three meeting places—a small one on the north side of town, the big one out where we live, and the old building downtown here. The old college up on the hill is now a university. This is their main campus, but they also offer classes at three other locations. We're members of an HMO that has doctors in five locations, but my primary-care physician is in a branch about a mile from where we live. Her office is next to a branch of the main hospital, so I've never been in the main hospital except to visit a couple of friends. Our older daughter is enrolled in a theological school out in California, but she is able to take all her classes on the east-side campus of First Church. That enables her to live with us and saves her a lot of money. We also look after her two children while she's in class or in the library."

As recently as the 1960s and 1970s, institutions expected their constituents to come to them. The location of the buildings that housed institutions also defined the urban landscape. In today's consumer-driven society, however, hospitals, lawyers, physicians, banks, and colleges now advertise for customers. The competition among various institutions to reach new generations has forced them to be more "customer-friendly."

One highly visible example of that is branch banking. In 1971 only 55 supermarkets housed a full-service branch of a bank. Fourteen years later that number had increased to only 210, but by 1997 4,400 supermarkets included a full-service branch bank.

In the 1920s, downtown churches established "outpost Sunday schools," many of which eventually evolved into self-governing, self-financing, self-expressing, and self-propagating congregations, out in the new residential subdivisions on the edge of the city. In the 1944–62 era, denominational systems planted new missions to reach those new residents. In addition, a fair number of congregations, both white and black, relocated their meeting place as they followed the migration of their members to better housing.

Today a growing number of congregations, when faced with the question, "Should we relocate or stay here at this sacred place?" answer, "Yes." They launch a capital funds campaign designed to (a) renovate the old building and (b) acquire the land for a second meeting place and the construction of that first unit of a three-stage building program on the new site. They continue as one congregation with one staff, one treasury, one membership roster, one governing board, and one name (it may be Bethany East and Bethany North or Trinity West and Trinity Central), but with three or four or five or six or seven or eight worship services every weekend and an open-ended commitment to continue to function as a two- (or three-) site congregation.

The success of these multisite ventures has changed the context for ministry. As recently as the 1980s, it was widely assumed that every Christian congregation included a worshiping community, one place where that community gathered, and one or more pastors.

A growing number of churches today are organized as a congregation of worshiping communities that meet at different times and places for different kinds of worship experiences. One version calls for a 5:00 P.M. Saturday worship service for families that include a child who still takes an afternoon nap; a 7:00 P.M. Saturday service for young adults in the 18 to 23 age bracket; an early Sunday morning service organized around the Lord's Supper; a nontraditional worship service held concurrently with a full-scale Sunday school; a late Sunday morning traditional worship service;

and the "Good News at Six O'clock" Sunday evening service; plus somewhere between five and two hundred other Sunday morning off-campus worship services designed to reach people who have zero interest in coming to an English-language worship service in that big and intimidating building that houses a congregation made up largely of people with whom these folks feel they have nothing in common. One of these off-campus worshiping communities is the creation of a ministry team consisting of a pastor and three to five volunteers. They offer a "seeker-sensitive," nontraditional service at ten o'clock Sunday morning in a remodeled storefront in a shopping center. The space is located between a drugstore open twenty-four hours a day and an office-supply store. Two years following that first service, they now average 160 at worship. Nearly all these worshipers have had no active church relationship since high school, and most are in the 25 to 35 age bracket. All are white and well over half have earned at least one college degree.

That same Sunday morning, teams of three to five volunteers are worshiping with off-campus communities in a variety of settings. One team is with residents of a mobile-home park; a second with a newly established Vietnamese community; a third with a group of single-parent mothers and their children in the community room of a large apartment complex; a fourth with a small group of recent immigrants from India; a fifth with residents of a nursing home; a sixth with recent immigrants from Mexico; a seventh with a group of high school youth in the community meeting room of a bank (the manager of that bank is one of the volunteers); the eighth team is worshiping in a room at the YMCA with mothers who have a husband in jail or prison; and a ninth with a group of undergraduates at a university ten miles from this congregation's meeting place.[13]

The most obvious consequence is that "church" is now being defined as people rather than as real estate.

Second, instead of sending money to hire others to do ministry on their behalf, these congregations are challenging, enlisting, training, and nurturing volunteers to reach people who would never come to that congregation's principal meeting place.

Third, instead of reporting how many dollars that congregation sent away for missions, the new reporting system asks four questions.

1. How many off-campus worshiping communities did this congregation include last year?
2. How many new ones were created this year?
3. What is the combined worship attendance of all these communities?
4. How does that compare with a year ago?

Fourth, perhaps the most interesting consequence is that several of these multisite congregations have discovered that their off-campus ministries are the most effective channels for reaching skeptics, agnostics, nonbelievers, inquirers, and people at the very earliest stage of their faith journey. The focus is on making new believers. Back at the ranch, at the "old" campus, the most effective ministry often is challenging believers to become disciples of Jesus Christ and equipping these disciples to do ministry.

Fifth, the staffing of these off-campus ministries is perhaps the most impressive evidence of the fact that when deeply committed laypersons are (a) challenged to be engaged in doing ministry and (b) equipped to carry out a specific ministry, they will respond.

Sixth, success breeds success. After the leaders experience the effectiveness of off-campus ministries, it is relatively easy to implement the goal of launching three to seven new worshiping communities every year. Few rarely grow to an average worship attendance beyond thirty-five. Perhaps one-third experience a life expectancy of fewer than five years. This means the leaders should think in terms of ministry with a passing parade of people rather than the creation of new permanent institutions.

Finally, from a financial perspective, this may be the most cost-effective approach to evangelism. In one congregation the annual expenditure to meet the costs of gathering an average of nearly 800 people for worship on the average weekend was $750,000 (exclusive of money sent away for missions and benevolences). The cost, including paid staff and building rentals, for twenty off-campus ministries with a combined average worship attendance of 565, was $120,000.

As your congregation designs its ministry plan for the twenty-first century, should off-campus ministries be included in that plan?

The Big Omission

At this point at least a few readers will object, "You've largely overlooked the most significant points of discontinuity with the past. The adults of today are not clones or carbon copies of the adults of the 1950s!"

That is a valid point! Demographics is destiny. Deaths and births do create the greatest degree of discontinuity with the past. William Jefferson Clinton was born in 1946, and he is a radically different leader than was Harry Truman, who was president of the United States from April 1945 to January 1953.

One way to minimize the impact of this passing parade of generations is to focus on ministries with adults born before 1945. Many congregations and several denominations have chosen that alternative.

This observer's defense is that my intent was not to write a book on demographic trends and the impact of those trends. That would be an even longer book. A bit of that did creep into this manuscript, but that is not the central focus of this book.

The scope and complexity of that theme can be illustrated by a few dozen statistics.

1. In 1991–94 inclusive, an annual average of 1.1 million legal immigrants were admitted into the United States, up from an annual average of 220,000 in 1951–54.

2. In 1951–54 two-thirds of the legal immigrants came from Europe; in 1991–94 only 13 percent of the legal immigrants in the United States came from Europe, while 37 percent came from Mexico, the Caribbean, and Central America, and another 31 percent came from Asia.

3. The proportion of the residents of the United States who were born in another country was 14.7 percent in 1910, 4.8 percent in 1970, and 9.3 percent in 1996, with 27.2 percent born in Mexico, 26.7 percent born in Asia, 16.9 percent born in Europe, 10.5 percent born in the Caribbean, and 9.9 percent born in Central America.

4. In March 1996, out of all American residents ages 25 and over, 30.8 percent of the naturalized citizens had earned a college degree, as had 23.6 percent of native-born Americans and 19.1 percent of the foreign-born residents who were not citizens.

5. The proportion of mothers in the United States who have completed high school rose from 62 percent in 1970 to 83 percent in 1990.

6. Ever since 1965, adults ages 65 and over have outnumbered teenagers in the American population.

7. Only 45 percent of the students who graduated from high school in 1982 and subsequently earned at least 10 college credits had earned a bachelor's degree by their thirtieth birthday.

8. The number of women who remarried after divorce or

widowhood was 370,000 in 1952, up from 186,000 in 1922, and passed a million in 1994.

9. The number of couples in an intercultural marriage (including Hispanic–non-Hispanic, but exclusive of Swedish-Norwegian) increased from 1.3 million in 1970 to 4.8 million in 1995, and 30 percent of the couples in an intercultural marriage in 1995 were black-white couples.

10. The number of unmarried couples living together with children 15 years of age and younger increased from 196,000 in 1970 to 1,319,000 in 1995.

11. The number of children born to unmarried women ages 20 and over increased from 48,000 in 1940 to 111,000 in 1955 to 860,000 in 1992.

12. The annual birth rate for unmarried white women ages 25 to 29 with 8 years or less of formal education was 257 per 1,000 white women in that age cohort in 1992, compared to 7.3 per 1,000 unmarried white women in that age bracket who had completed four years of college (for unmarried black women ages 25 to 29, the comparable birth rates were 79 and 46).

13. The proportion of all women, ages 25 to 29, currently not married increased from 13 percent in 1965 to 21 percent in 1975 to 41 percent in 1992.

14. The annual birth rates for unmarried women ages 25 to 29 increased from 34 per 1,000 women in 1980 to 56.5 in 1992.

15. The number of children living in a household headed by a grandparent increased from 935,000 in 1990 to 1.8 million in 1997.

16. In 1950 only 4 percent of babies born in the United States were born to an unmarried mother; by 1997 that proportion had grown to 32 percent.

17. The number of Americans enrolled in tae kwon do classes was 6.3 million in 1997, up from 1.6 million in 1990, thanks to the search by parents for help in teaching self-esteem, discipline, and obedience.

18. The number of farms in the United States dropped from 6.8 million in 1935 to 5.1 million in 1955 to 1.7 million in 1997.

19. The number of farms covering 50 to 179 acres plummeted from 2.1 million in 1950 to 1.5 million in 1959 to slightly over 500,000 in 1997.

20. The proportion of two-parent families with children living at home in which both parents were employed in the labor force rose from 40 percent in 1970 to 60 percent in 1990.

21. The number of married couples living together with at least one of their own children under age 18 at home increased from 23.8 million in 1962 to 25.3 million in 1995, but the number of married couples living together *without* any of their own children under age 18 at home increased from 16.7 million in 1962 to 28.6 million in 1995.

22. In the early 1920s 10 percent of all widowed or divorced women, ages 15 to 54, remarried in any one year. That annual rate of remarriages dropped to 6 percent in the early 1930s, peaked at nearly 17 percent in 1966–68, but was down to 11 percent in the late 1980s.

23. The life expectancy of the white, 40-year-old American male in 1920 was 30 years and 31 for the 40-year-old white American female. By 1993 those life expectancies had increased to 36 and 41 years respectively.

24. The number of live births in the United States was between 2.9 million and 3.2 million in 1914, 1915, 1916, 1917, 1918, 1920, 1921, 1923, 1924, 1925, 1942, 1943, 1944, 1973, 1974, 1975, and 1976. By contrast, the number of live births in the United States was between 3.9 million and 4.3 million in 1952, 1953, 1954, 1955, 1956, 1957, 1958, 1959, 1960, 1961, 1962, 1963, 1964, 1988, 1989, 1990, 1991, 1992, 1993, 1994, 1995, and 1996.

25. When asked their ancestry in 1990, 60 million Americans claimed a German ancestry, 39 million Irish, 33

million English, 24 million African, 15 million Italian, 12 million Mexican, 10.3 million French, 9.3 million Polish, 8.7 million American Indian, and 6.2 million Dutch. (Many claimed two or more nationality heritages.)

26. The number of women giving birth to their first child after the mother's fortieth birthday increased from 3 per 10,000 in the age 40 to 44 cohort in 1970 to 14 per 10,000 in 1995.

27. For women ages 30 to 34 the number of first births was 70 per 10,000 women in 1970 and 229 per 10,000 in 1995.

28. The median level of educational attainment of the American population, ages 25 and over, jumped from 8.6 years in 1940 to 12.2 years in 1970 to nearly 13 years in 1997.

29. The proportion of the American population who had completed at least four years of college tripled from 7.7 percent in 1960 to 23 percent in 1995.

30. The number of five-year-olds enrolled in kindergarten increased from 786,000 in 1930 to 2,136,000 in 1950 to 4,050,000 in 1995.

31. The number of three-year-olds and four-year-olds enrolled in nursery school more than doubled from 1.5 million in 1970 to 3.8 million in 1996.

32. The number of public one-teacher elementary schools dropped from 149,282 in 1930 to 59,652 in 1950 to 20,213 in 1960 to slightly over a thousand in 1979.

33. Between 1980 and 1995 the Euro-American population of the United States increased by 12.3 million, the Hispanic and Latino population increased by 12.6 million, the African American population increased by 6.5 million, and the Asian-Pacific Islander population increased by 5.5 million.

34. The annual number of births per 1,000 women ages 15 to 44 dropped from 278 in 1800 to 194 in 1850 to 111

in 1924 to 76 in 1936 and then climbed to 123 in 1957 before dropping to 68 in 1993.

35. The death rate for infants has plunged from 162 per 1,000 births in 1900 to 78 in 1926 to 35 in 1949 to 7.2 in 1996.

36. The population of the United States age 60 and over doubled between 1930 and 1955 and doubled again between 1955 and 1991 to 42.3 million and stood at 45 million in 1998.

37. The 888,000 square miles of land area in the 672 counties that are located in a coastal watershed cover one fourth of the land area of the United States and include 53 percent of the residents.

38. The proportion of Americans, ages 5 to 19, enrolled in school climbed from 47.2 percent in 1850 to 54 percent in 1890 to 75 percent in 1940 to 88.6 percent in 1960 to 93 percent in 1991.

39. Enrollment in Catholic elementary schools climbed from 1.8 million in 1919–20 to a peak of slightly over 4.5 million in 1963–64 and gradually decreased to 1.9 million in 1990–91, while enrollment in non-Catholic private elementary schools has climbed from 350,000 in 1963–64 to 2.2 million in 1990–91, much of that increase being in Protestant schools.

40. The number of bachelor's degrees conferred by American institutions of higher education (including first professional degrees) quadrupled from 11,932 in 1874–75 to 48,622 in 1919–20, a period of forty-five years, reached a temporary peak thirty years later at 432,058 in 1949–50, and has been running between 1 million and 1.2 million each year in the 1990s.

41. The number of single-parent fathers living with children under 18 at home quintupled from slightly under 400,000 in 1970 to nearly 2 million in 1997, while the number of families headed by a single-parent mother with chil-

dren under 18 at home nearly doubled from 5.4 million in 1980 to 10 million in 1997.

42. The number of women, ages 65 and over, living alone quadrupled from 2 million in 1960 to nearly 8 million in 1997, while the number of men, ages 65 and over, living alone nearly tripled from 853,000 in 1960 to 2.4 million in 1997.

43. The number of persons housed in correctional institutions dropped from 346,000 in 1960 to 328,000 in 1970 and then quintupled to 1.6 million in 1997.

44. The number of mobile homes occupied on a year-round basis was 5.6 million in 1993, up from slightly over 4 million in 1979, while in the same period the number of occupied housing units in buildings containing five or more units doubled from 9.2 million to 18.2 million, but the number of occupied detached single-family homes increased by only 23 percent from 49 million to 60 million.

For those who have been able to read this far, those changes represent 44 possibilities to expand or to redefine the ministry of your congregation.

5
WHAT ARE THE CONSEQUENCES?

Changes have consequences. One of the keys to a happy life is a willingness and an ability to live with the future consequences of current actions. One of the keys to effective planning for the twenty-first century by both congregations and denominational agencies is the capability to understand and adjust to the consequences of discontinuity with the past. What are the most significant consequences of the many changes described in the first four chapters?

A useful way to begin to respond to that question may be to reflect on it from six different perspectives—congregational, ministerial, parishioner, call committee, denominational, and the theological school.

A Congregational Perspective

From a congregational perspective the number one consequence of the various fundamental points of discontinuity with the past discussed in the previous two chapters is an unprecedented level of competition among the churches for new members. As recently as the 1970s many congregations could count on inherited denominational loyalties, the convenient location of their meeting place, kinship and friendship ties, and/or the characteristics of the members (social class, race, nationality, occupation, age, marital status, and the like) as attractions that would lure replacements for those members who moved away, dropped out, or died. Today church shopping is the norm, not the exception. A growing number of adults looking for a worshiping community that will be sensitive and responsive to their religious, personal, and family needs are willing to spend months visiting one congregation after another until they find what they seek. The younger the church seekers and/or the higher their income level and/or the more times they have changed churches and/or the more formal education they have enjoyed and/or the more intentional they are about their faith journey and/or the greater the distance between their current place of residence and where they attended high school and/or the more times they have changed their address, the easier it is for them to church shop. Add to that the remarkable recent increase in the number of interfaith and interdenominational marriages and remarriages and the rapid rise in the number of nondenominational congregations, and it is easy to understand why competition for future members tops this list of the consequences of discontinuity.

A second consequence from a congregational perspective overlaps the first. Which congregations have an edge on this competition for future members? One answer is those with a clearly defined identity or community image based on what that church is doing in ministry.

In the 1950s the identity of a particular congregation usually rested on (1) the denominational affiliation; (2) the real estate; (3) the location (open country, small town, suburban, central city); (4) the social class, race, national origins, language, or ethnic heritage of the members (Swedish Lutheran, Italian Methodist, etc.); (5) the visibility and role of the pastor as a community leader ("Oh! You're a member of Doctor Harrison's church?"); and (6) the size of the congregation.

Today three of the most widely used variables in defining

a congregation's identity are (a) the ethnic composition of the membership, (b) what it is doing in ministry, and (c) its theological stance. "That's the church with the biggest youth program in town." "That's an Afrocentric congregation." "That's a charismatic congregation." "They have the number one ministry with families with young children." "They have more adults engaged in serious in-depth Bible study than any other church around here." "I don't understand how they are able to do it, but they offer six different worship services every week." "That is a theologically very liberal church." "That is a high commitment parish." "They have the biggest youth ministry of any church in town."

A third consequence is the natural and predictable product of the passage of time. Most new religious movements or denominations or congregations originally were founded as covenant communities. High expectations were projected of anyone who sought to become a full member. As the decades roll by, the normal institutional tendency is for that organization to drift in the direction of becoming a voluntary association that projects relatively low expectations of members.

A common example is the congregation founded in 1880. Ten years later it reported 70 members and an average worship attendance of 85. By 1925 the reported membership had grown to 220 and worship attendance averaged 175. Thirty years later those numbers were 330 and 260. Four decades later the membership had dropped to 290 and church attendance averaged 135. Over the years it gradually had become easier to maintain one's standing as a full member. What had begun as a covenant community had evolved into a voluntary association. The high threshold into full membership had become a low threshold.

In several religious traditions the requirements and rituals for becoming a full member had been designed by men long since dead and had been created for a covenant community. Today most congregations in those traditions act like low expectation, voluntary associations, and the expectations articulated in the vows of membership are largely ignored.

This inconsistency between the promises in the vows and the behavior patterns of most of the new members often evokes this comment from the pillars who have been active and committed members for decades: "If all our members took their vows seriously, our pews would be filled and we would have a surplus of money and volunteers!"

A realistic response explains, "Those vows were designed for a high commitment, covenant-community type of church, and we are now a low expectation, voluntary association. By definition people joining a voluntary association assume they have the right to come in on their own terms and at their own pace and thus retain the right to regulate their own degree of participation. In the covenant community the group sets the standards, and everyone seeking to become a part of that covenant community agrees to meet those standards and fulfill the expectations set by that group."

A fourth consequence overlaps the first three. This is the emergence of large numbers of nondenominational churches. While they admit to many disadvantages when compared to denominationally affiliated congregations, their advantages give them an edge in this competition for younger adults. One advantage is that since no one joins because of a previous denominational affiliation, these churches have to be exceptionally sensitive and responsive to the religious and personal needs of people on a self-identified faith journey.[1]

A fifth consequence is one that is seldom discussed in these terms. Which congregations have an edge in this increasingly competitive ecclesiastical environment? From this observer's perspective, it is clearly those churches that proclaim the gospel of Jesus Christ with certainty. The absence of ambiguity in the teaching and preaching stands in marked contrast to those who preface many statements with words resembling these: "While several scholars contend this is the way it was, a growing number of younger scholars offer this interpretation of what happened." In today's world people come to church in search of certainty, not in a quest for more knowledge.

Certainty in the teaching and preaching is compatible with the high expectation church. Ambiguity in teaching and preaching is compatible with the low expectation, voluntary association in which all members are encouraged to create their own belief system and define their own level of participation.

A sixth consequence also is a product of the enhanced competition and has two facets. One can be summarized by the old saying, "Them that has, gits." Those congregations that are large enough to enjoy the luxury of discretionary resources, to secure the leadership of an exceptionally gifted and long-tenured pastor, to be structured with a variety of inviting entry points for newcomers, to offer at least two high-quality worship experiences every weekend, and to encourage an emphasis on creating a new tomorrow rather than struggling to perpetuate yesterday are better equipped to attract and assimilate the people who project high expectations of a church, who expect a range of attractive choices, who assume this church will offer a relevant response to their religious needs, who seek a variety of opportunities to enjoy a sense of community, who make high quality a priority, and who prefer a church that projects a clearly defined identity.

In summary, the large churches are growing in size. In several denominations, for example, an average worship attendance of 2,800 was required to be ranked as the largest congregation in that denomination in the mid-1960s. Today an average worship attendance of 4,500 or 5,500 or 8,500 or 14,000 is reported by the largest church of that denomination.

At the other end of the size spectrum, many of the 75,000 Protestant congregations averaging 20 to 50 at worship may find these changes reassuring. The hunger of many Christians for intimacy, for being a part of a genuine caring community, for the opportunity to know that their feelings and needs are being understood, for a sense of continuity with the past, for the comfort of knowing they are being heard when they speak, and for the joy of worshiping God with people who share a similar belief system can best be satisfied in the small congregation.[2]

The small churches that are able and willing to concentrate their resources on what they do best have a promising future.

From a congregational perspective, a radically different consequence of this discontinuity is a shrinkage in the number of middle-sized congregations averaging 85 to 200 at worship. They are too small to compete for new members with the big congregations and too large, too impersonal, and too complicated to compete for those who prefer a small, intimate, and caring fellowship. The demand for gifted, energetic, creative, visionary, and skilled pastors greatly exceeds the supply, so that also handicaps these middle-sized churches as they seek to compete with the megachurches for future members.

It is easy to declare that the competition among the churches for potential future members is far greater than it was in the 1950s or even the 1960s. It also is easy to point out that a natural consequence is that the names of thousands of middle-sized congregations are now being added to that list of endangered species.

For many people, however, it is far more difficult to accept those descriptive statements about contemporary reality as useful or even as legitimate topics of conversation. Those who are ideologically committed to intercongregational cooperation, to the unity of the Christian church, and to the geographical definition of the parish may find these observations one inch this side of heresy. To them these descriptive statements appear to affirm proselytizing and sheep stealing and may be used as evidence to prove the devil is alive and at work in the world. Only Satan could approve competition among congregations for future members! To refer to a congregation averaging close to 200 at worship as a candidate for the endangered species list is clearly giving aid and comfort to the enemy!

A more productive response, however, may be to nod affirmatively and comment, "This helps me understand why it is far more difficult to be a parish pastor today than it was forty years ago."

A Ministerial Perspective

In a provocative essay, a journalist has pointed out that it is far more difficult to be the successful manager of a major league baseball team today than it was a few decades earlier. In the old days a good manager picked the best lineup to play that game, wrote the names in the most productive order on the scorecard, and sent the appropriate pinch hitter to bat for the pitcher at the crucial time. Today, declared Mark Starr, understanding the fundamentals of baseball is only one of several qualities required in a good baseball manager. That array of skills and gifts now includes concerns such as motivation, media, marketing, multiculturalism, listening skills, leadership abilities, and the ability to live with huge egos.[3]

The parallel is that it was far easier to be an effective parish pastor in the 1950s than in the 1990s. One part of the explanation for that statement is the increased competition for new members. Another is the distrust of institutions. A third has been the erosion of denominational identities by the success of ecumenism and the attractiveness of the large nondenominational congregations.

A fourth is the skill required to choose wisely from among that exploding abundance of resources now available to pastors and congregations. Perhaps the most important single factor is the rising level of expectations people bring to church. The emergence of the consumer-driven economy discussed in the second chapter has raised the level of expectations people bring when they shop for a house, a motor vehicle, an airplane ticket, a school for their children, a motel room, a health-insurance program, a job, or a new church home.

Perhaps the most subtle consequence for parish pastors is expressed in the distinction between knowledge and skill. From the 1870s through the 1950s, the dominant assumption was that a head full of knowledge was the most valuable asset for a person responding to God's call to be a parish pastor. One consequence was the publication of thousands of books on theology and biblical interpretation, but relatively few on leadership. Another was the requirement of a seminary degree for ordination in many denominations.

The last third of the twentieth century brought a growing recognition that skill in leadership, in effective communication, and in interpersonal relationships ranks ahead of knowledge as an asset in the pastoral ministry. One consequence is that the pastor of the congregation averaging 300 at worship today is more likely to be a seminary graduate than the founding pastor of the congregation averaging 3,000 at worship. A second consequence is that many pastors own more books on how to do ministry than on doctrine. A third is that the focus in continuing-education experiences for pastors has changed from acquiring more knowledge about Scripture and doctrine to enhancing leadership skills.

Another consequence, which some ministers will declare is positive while others will view it in negative terms, reflects the growing demand for specialists. While a large proportion of ministers today are comfortable as generalists, others are comfortable in a specialized role. That long list includes ministers of missions, hospital chaplains, specialists in small-group ministries, executive pastors, pastoral counselors, ministers of prayer, builders of learning communities, parish consultants, ministers of community outreach, worship leaders, youth pastors, and program directors. Most of those positions did not exist in the 1950s.

Another consequence, which reflects the changing nature of the total American labor force, is the increase in part-time jobs. A reasonable guess is that by the year 2025 at least 135,000 Protestant congregations will be served by a part-time minister. A shrinking number will be the full-time ordained ministers who are part-time in each of two or three congregations. A growing number will be lay ministers. A significant number will be seminary graduates who also (a) have a full-time secular job or (b) are full-time home-makers or (c) are early retirees from the secular labor force.

Another 100,000 will be part-time specialists on the staff of large congregations. Some will have secular employment, many will be homemakers, while others simply prefer part-time work, and a fair number will be young retirees.

For several thousand full-time program staff members, both lay and clergy, the most significant consequence is the shift from being a soloist or generalist to becoming a member of a program team that includes two to twenty lay volunteers. Currently the most highly visible example of this is the worship team of two or three paid staff persons and five to fifteen volunteers. For many full-time professionals this means being the leader of one team and an active member of two or three other teams.

When examined in a larger context, this reflects a huge change in the sources and context for building interpersonal relationships. In the old days the associate minister socialized with the associate pastors from four or five other congregations. Today the successor socializes with four or five other team members or team leaders from within that large church.

Likewise, back in the 1950s many pastors often identified with and felt a strong sense of loyalty to their regional judicatory (presbytery, diocese, synod, conference, district, or region) and socialized with fellow pastors from that regional judicatory. To a significant degree, that reflected the fact that life was organized on (a) relationships based on geographical proximity and (b) the differences that separate "us" from "them."

Today interpersonal relationships are far more likely to reflect what ministers have in common rather than geographical proximity or the lines of demarcation based on doctrinal differences. One consequence is the emergence of a variety of caucuses within each of several denominational systems. One is the caucus of Latino pastors. A second is the caucus of evangelical pastors in the theologically liberal denomination. A third is the caucus of town and country pastors. A fourth is the gay and lesbian caucus. A fifth is the African American caucus. A sixth is the Korean pastors' caucus. A seventh is the caucus of senior pastors of very large congregations. An eighth is the lay-clergy coalition with an anti-headquarters agenda.

One consequence is that the pastor who is actively involved in two or three of these caucuses may have little time for or interest in involvement in the official denominational system. Paralleling this is another trend discussed earlier. In the 1960s a pastor might share two professional passions. One was a passion for the life and ministry of the congregation served by that pastor. The other might be that pastor's involvement in the Civil Rights movement or the ecumenical movement or some other single-issue movement. For the busy pastor this often meant the denominational system ranked no higher than third as a place to invest discretionary time and energy.

The emergence of networks in the 1970s and 1980s brought a new place to invest those discretionary resources. For many senior ministers or large congregations, that network of peers ranks up there with congregation and family (or in a few cases family and congregation) as the most attractive places to invest time and energy. The denominational system ranks somewhere between fourth and seventeenth as an attractive alternative for the investment of those scarce resources.

For many parish pastors the most threatening consequence of the discontinuity with the past is in the redefinition of the qualities required to be an effective parish pastor. For at least ten generations the ideal parish pastor was (1) a godly person; (2) a committed disciple of Jesus Christ; (3) a loving shepherd who excelled in caring for individuals; (4) an inspiring preacher; (5) an effective teacher; (6) a reasonably competent administrator; (7) a persuasive evangelist; (8) a person of good moral character; (9) a loyal member of that denominational family; (10) a respected community leader; (11) an adult who enjoyed ministering to children, youth, and mature adults; and (12) a person who enjoyed a frugal lifestyle and a long work week.

The order of importance of those qualities varied with the size and personality of the congregation. The typical small congregation usually placed a high priority on 2, 8, and 10 while the very large church ranked 4, 6, and 9 near the top of the list.

Today at least 30 percent of the churches want a pastor who also excels as an entrepreneurial leader, but fewer than 10 percent of all parish pastors are both comfortable and competent in that role.

To make it even more threatening, the decisions made by that rapidly growing number of church shoppers suggest the "rewards" go to those who (a) accept it is now a highly competitive environment in that quest for future members and

(b) are able and willing to seek to excel as competitors in that environment. Whatever happened to the expectation that faithfulness and obedience would be rewarded, in this life as well as in heaven?

A Parishioner's Perspective

One of the most significant consequences of discontinuity with the past is the expectations parishioners bring to church. In the 1950s many parishioners expected their church would provide them with a well-prepared and helpful sermon once or twice a week, good Christian music, a well-organized Sunday school, a balanced church budget, a relevant ministry with teenagers, a healthy emphasis on missions, and opportunities for people to give of their time, talents, and loyalty. By the late 1950s a small but growing number of parishioners expected their minister also would be a competent pastoral counselor.

New generations of parishioners bring expectations that the church will be prepared to offer help on a huge variety of religious, personal, and vocational concerns; to meet them at the current stage of their faith journey and help them progress on to the next stage; to affirm their preference to come into that congregation on their own terms and at their own pace; to help them rear their children; to invite them to volunteer on the basis of each individual's gifts rather than in response to the institutional needs of that congregation; to provide a broad range of choices in high-quality ministries; to enable them to become a member of a genuinely caring community; and to guarantee a conveniently located, vacant, and safe parking space whenever they arrive.

They expect a relevant, high-quality, and meaningful response to their religious needs, and they expect attractive choices where they can enjoy a sense of community within the context of all of those choices.

When the parishioner of the 1950s decided to go to a movie, one alternative was to go to the closest motion-picture theater and watch that movie. A second was to travel to a more distant single-screen theater. A third option was not to go to the movies that evening.

The motion-picture industry taught the moviegoers of that era that they were entitled to a limited range of choices. Most of the patrons of that theater either walked or parked on the street or paid a dime to a quarter to park in a municipal parking facility.

Today the thirty-nine-year-old adult child of that parishioner has more choices. One is to travel to that nearby twelve- (or twenty- or thirty-) screen motion-picture theater and choose from among a broad range of movies. In a few families the husband will go to one, the wife to a second, the fourteen-year-old daughter will choose a third, and the eleven-year-old son will pick a fourth movie. Afterward they go together for refreshments.

A second choice is to choose a different multiscreen theater. A third alternative is to watch a movie that evening on television. A fourth is to rent a videotape. A fifth is to not watch a movie that night. The motion-picture industry has been teaching younger generations that they are entitled to a wide range of choices, including convenient and free off-street parking.

The church that is seeking to reach and serve the parents of that thirty-nine-year-old may offer a Sunday morning schedule that begins with worship followed by Sunday school followed by a second worship service that is a carbon copy of the early service. That is consistent with the schedule of the single-screen motion-picture theater of the 1950s that showed the same feature at seven o'clock and again at nine.

Another church that is seeking to compete with several other congregations to reach that thirty-nine-year-old often has designed a four-period schedule for Sunday morning. The first period includes a worship service centered on Holy Communion plus a couple of adult classes that may meet for two periods of time. The second period includes two concurrent worship services in two different rooms, one traditional and one nontraditional, plus a couple of one-hour adult classes, plus a nursery and one or two classes for teenagers. The third period consists of Sunday school classes for all ages. The fourth includes a traditional worship service, perhaps with a different preacher or speaker, and a nontraditional worship experience that differs in several respects from its counterpart at the earlier hour, plus at least a couple of adult classes and at least one class for youth.

That thirty-nine-year-old person and spouse may arrive near the end of that first period, park in the church-owned lot, and enjoy ten to twenty minutes of socializing with friends over coffee in the huge narthex. The husband and fourteen-year-old daughter go to the traditional worship service while the wife and son go to the nontraditional service. After worship, the family is reunited in the huge narthex or hall and the parents go off to their class together while the children go to their classes.

This is in addition to a long list of study groups, prayer cells, choirs, classes, volunteer teams, youth events, children's ministries, and servant activities scheduled for the remaining six and one-half days of the week.

The basic generalization is that the more high-quality and attractive choices a congregation can offer that family of church shoppers, the more likely they will return next week.

In the 1950s that was described as sheep stealing. Today it is described as competition. One of the subtle consequences is that the loyal member born before 1940 is upset or baffled when a longtime member becomes dissatisfied and quietly departs to worship with a different congregation in that same community. The younger member, who was reared in a culture overflowing with choices, shrugs off that departure as normal and completely acceptable.

In summary, many of the parishioners born after World War II have been taught they have a right to expect high quality; a wide range of attractive choices; inspiring, challenging, and relevant sermons; at least one high-energy worship experience every weekend; effective visual communication; a vacant parking space at a convenient location; at least one worship experience every weekend organized around their preference in music; opportunities to volunteer on the basis of gifts, passion, skills, and experience rather than on the need to fill an empty slot in that congregation's volunteer network; integrity and accountability in the financial administration of that congregation; the challenge to move to an advanced stage in their faith journey and the resources that will make that a rewarding experience; a variety of opportunities to meet and make new friends; a small group where they can enjoy participation in a caring community; a guarantee that nearly everyone on the staff can call them correctly by name; a conviction that responding to their religious needs is a high priority there; and an unreserved affirmation of the power of intercessory prayer.

In addition, most expect that they are free to come in on their own terms at their own pace, that there is no urgency or pressure to become a full member, and that they are free to leave when they choose without anyone attempting to make them feel guilty about their departure.

Do you see this expansion in the range of choices offered to people and the higher quality demanded by people a source of hope or a cause for alarm?

A Call Committee's Perspective

Grace Church was founded in 1922 on the far east side of the city. Today the suburban ring extends another eight miles beyond the 40,000-square-foot parcel of land that has served as the meeting place for this congregation since 1924. The number of people living within seven miles of the Grace Church property has doubled since 1970.

Grace Church peaked in size with an average worship attendance of 385 in 1951 and last year averaged 240 at worship. The seventh pastor in the congregation's history arrived fourteen years ago and will be retiring in two months.

For this discussion let us assume that one hundred candidates will receive serious consideration to become the eighth pastor. Every one of the hundred (a) is under fifty-two years of age, (b) has earned the Master of Divinity degree from an accredited seminary, (c) has at least eight years' experience in the parish ministry (and twenty candidates currently are serving as associate ministers in congregations larger in size than Grace Church), and (d) has passed the preliminary screening process.

How many of those one hundred candidates probably will turn out to be a good-to-excellent match to the needs of Grace Church?

If the year is 1959, the answer could be forty. If the year is 1979, the answer probably is closer to twenty. If the year is 1999, the answer may be somewhere between three and seven.

Seven generalizations provide the foundations for those estimates.

1. The longer the congregation has been in existence, the more difficult it is to produce a good match between the needs of the congregation and the gifts, skills, experience, wisdom, and belief system of the next pastor.

2. The more time that has elapsed since that congregation peaked in size, the more difficult it is to produce a good match.

3. The larger the size of the congregation—and Grace

Church is larger than 85 percent of all the congregations in American Protestantism—the more difficult it is to find a good match.

4. The larger the number of predecessors, the more difficult it is to produce a good match.

5. The faster the rate of population growth, the more difficult it is to produce a good match.

6. The greater the competition among the churches for future members, the more difficult it is to produce a good match. (The number of congregations competing with Grace Church for future members has tripled since 1970.)

7. The closer we are to the beginning of the twenty-first century, (a) the greater the number and variety of expectations people bring to church, (b) the higher the level of complexity in congregational life, and (c) the more difficult it is to be an effective parish pastor.

These comments all add up to one statement: The burden on the committee searching for a new pastor is far heavier and far more complicated today than it was in the 1950s or the 1970s. So, you have been asked to serve on the committee that is to search for a new pastor. What do you do?

1. Switch your membership to another church.

2. Say no, and seek an easier assignment such as chairing the finance committee or working with high school youth or serving on the special task force that has been assigned the responsibility of persuading the sixty-three-year-old choir director to choose early retirement.

3. Buy time and skill. Urge that the next step should be to bring in an experienced intentional interim minister who will (a) make sure all the necessary endings have been completed for closure on the last pastor's ministry, (b) help the congregation shift its orientation from the past to the future, (c) work with a long-range planning committee in hearing and responding to what God is calling this congregation to be and

to do in the next chapter of its history, and (d) articulate several dozen questions[4] the search committee should reflect on and pray about before beginning to build a list of potential candidates.

4. Buy experience. Look for a person who has helped several dozen other congregations through the process of bidding farewell to one minister and identifying the successor. This may be an experienced denominational staffer or it may be a private consultant or it may be a layperson who chaired the search process in a similar type of congregation.

5. Agree to serve on one condition. That condition is that all members of this committee will be the cream-of-the-crop, top-quality, truly gifted, and highly competent individuals. The top-quality people usually are comfortable with top-quality candidates. The second-raters tend to be more comfortable bringing on board third-rate candidates.[5]

6. Agree to serve and insist that before beginning to build that list of potential candidates, the search committee will (a) identify the major points of discontinuity with the past that have surfaced in recent years in the life and ministry of this congregation; (b) discuss the present and future consequences of that discontinuity; (c) identify the probable points of discontinuity which the next three to seven years will bring and the probable consequences; (d) agree whether the next pastor should be a successor who will carry on what the predecessor was doing or a transitional leader who is equipped to help lead this congregation into a new chapter or stage in its history or a transformational leader who will help lead this congregation in a radical redefinition of its purpose, role, identity, and mission; (e) formulate a few dozen statements describing the belief system, the current ministry plan, the current constituency, and the congregational culture and priorities in the allocation of resources that can be used to focus the discussions with candidates.

7. Agree to serve on that search committee, but with one

major reservation. That reservation is to demand clarity on the assignment of the committee. What is our primary task? To find someone to fill the vacancy? To review the work load on the paid staff and design a new staff configuration? To find someone who will help us recreate yesterday? To design the staff configuration that will be appropriate for a new tomorrow? To look for a pastor who can help us implement the strategy designed by our long-range planning committee? To identify the staff members who should be asked to resign before we begin the process of looking for a new pastor? To identify critical staff responsibilities that are not being fulfilled and design a new staff configuration that promises to solve that problem? To study the advantages and disadvantages of going from full-time to part-time paid staff? To consider replacing the position of senior minister with a leadership team of three to five persons (pastor, executive pastor, program director) and seek someone who can help to build and lead that team?

8. Choose the easy road and challenge each candidate with this statement: "We are looking for a minister who is an inspiring leader and who is equipped to lead us into a new day. We really don't care where you lead us, just lead! We're a blank slate waiting for the new minister to write on us." Recommend the candidate who articulates the most attractive future scenario. It is easier to be passive than active, but you will have to live with the results of that passivity.

No one will challenge the assertion that the task of a call committee is more difficult today than it was forty years ago. Do these growing differences that distinguish one congregation from all others also make it more rewarding?

A Denominational Perspective

For a couple of hundred years, the central purposes of denominational systems were largely confined to these eight:

(1) credential clergy; (2) create and support a sense of community among the ministers and transmit to each new generation of pastors the values, belief system, culture, traditions, and polity of that denominational system; (3) enlist missionaries and raise money for their support on other continents; (4) start new churches where needed; (5) resource congregations with hymnals, Sunday school curricula, and other printed materials; (6) preserve doctrinal purity and combat heresy; (7) create and raise money to support new Christian institutions such as colleges, theological schools, orphanages, homes, publishing houses, camps, and hospitals; and (8) schedule and administer denominational rallies to inspire the believers, convert the nonbelievers, and reinforce denominational loyalties. After World War II an increasing number of denominations began to offer congregations expert help in fund-raising, Christian education, youth ministries, women's ministries, and other specialized services.

Today denominational agencies are expected to provide a broad array of sophisticated and relevant resources to congregations; to serve as effective advocates of social justice; to plant new missions; to make disciples of nonbelievers; to revitalize dying churches; to provide challenging continuing-education opportunities for both clergy and laity; to administer a fiscally sound pension system for clergy; to help pastors in their search for a new pastorate; to offer skilled counseling services to troubled pastors; to collect and redistribute money; to provide a platform for those who are advocating a particular cause; to enlist, train, screen, send, and support missionaries to all parts of the world; to financially support institutions founded in the nineteenth century and the early decades of the twentieth century; to preserve the family farm; to resource and revitalize inner-city neighborhoods; to provide employment opportunities for adults; to influence governmental policies on immigration, the death penalty, abortion, foreign policy, education, taxation, gambling, and social welfare; to maintain community centers; to create new Christian institutions in response to new needs; to arrange mission trips for church members; to promote ecumenism; to combat drug use; to provide high-quality child care at affordable fees; to enlist and screen candidates for the ministry; to produce audiotapes and videotapes for congregational use; to schedule and administer large denominational rallies; to maintain a denominational publishing house; to credential clergy and combat heresy; to create new opportunities for the laity to be engaged in doing ministry; to financially subsidize congregations that are relocating their meeting place and/or expanding their physical facilities; to administer a health-insurance program; to subsidize small churches in order to provide employment for a surplus of clergy; to build and operate retirement centers; to create multicultural congregations; to publish a denominational magazine or newspaper; to conduct continuing-education events for pastors over the Internet; and to build broad-based support for denominational proclamations on divisive issues of public policy.

One consequence of this overloaded agenda in some regional and national judicatories is to attempt to please everyone by endorsing dozens of priorities. This is reflected in the denominational budget. Instead of dividing a million dollars in missions money between the two top missional priorities, that million dollars is divided among several dozen priorities, with most receiving between $500 and $15,000 while one or two are allocated an amount that will make a difference.

A second consequence of that overloaded agenda is that at some point in the 1955–90 era every mainline Protestant denomination decided to cut back dramatically on new church development. For most the decrease in the number of new missions launched each year was in the 60 to 90 percent range from the peak years of the 1950s and 1960s.

New church development was replaced as a high priority in denominational agencies by the need to resource denominational mergers, to finance new urban ministries, to create and support a variety of special interest groups, to fund social justice ministries, to promote ecumenism, to keep dying institutions alive, to resource pastors, and to subsidize theological schools.

Among the consequences of those decisions to cut back on new church development were (1) a shrinking in the number of members, (2) an increase in the median age of the members, (3) a decrease in the proportion of all members from among the generations born after 1955, (4) an increase in the proportion of congregations averaging fewer than a hundred at worship, and (5) the creation of a vacuum to be filled by newer denominations and the independent churches as they started most of the new churches founded since 1970.

A third response to that overloaded agenda is being followed by a small but growing number of regional judicatories. One version devotes 70 to 90 percent of that judicatory's resources to a single goal: enabling congregations to fulfill the Great Commission. A second version is to allocate one-third to one-half of the budget to resourcing congregations, one-third to planting new missions, and allowing the various interest groups to fight over the remaining 15 to 35 percent of the financial resources.

A fourth response is for the regional judicatory to raise substantial amounts of money every year from user fees, individual donors, bequests, income from investments held in trust by that regional judicatory, and family foundations to be used in (a) challenging congregations to expand their ministry through matching grants and/or (b) funding new ministries.

The changes discussed in earlier chapters help to explain why many people believe denominational systems should be added to the list of endangered institutional species.

One reason is distrust of large and distant institutions. A second is the preference of many adults born after 1955 for independent churches. A third is the national shift toward local control, which in ecclesiastical terms means either strengthening the role of the regional judicatory or complete congregational self-autonomy. A fourth is that growing number of very large congregations where none of the leaders see any value added by maintaining a denominational affiliation. A fifth is the shift in the place where congregations turn for resources as described in chapter 1.

A sixth reason for this "endangered" status is the erosion of the systems for transmitting denominational loyalties from one generation to the next. In the 1950s many young people spent a week at a denominational summer camp that helped reinforce denominational loyalty. Today youngsters go on a two- or three-week-vacation trip with their parents, and many teenagers hold summer jobs. In the 1950s congregations used denominationally produced materials in Sunday school and other teaching ministries, and that helped to transmit denominational loyalties. Fifty years ago people were more likely to find a spouse from within their own religious tradition. Up through the 1960s the local women's organization usually was organized around supporting denominational missions, and that reinforced denominational loyalties. Today women's ministries are more likely to be organized around the needs and concerns of women than around supporting denominational causes. In the 1950s the denominational magazines were advocates of denominational goals and programs. Today they are more likely to be critics of the denomination's goals. Once upon a time candidates for the parish ministry attended theological schools created and supported by that denomination. Today they are more likely to attend a nearby nondenominational school or one affiliated with a different religious tradition. Once upon a time missionaries on furlough stayed overnight in the homes of church members and offered young people a walking model of what their denomination was doing in missions. Today itinerating missionaries are more likely to spend the night in a motel. These examples illustrate a few of the ways the old systems for the transmission of denominational loyalties have been eroded but not replaced by new systems.

A seventh reason for suggesting that traditional denominational systems belong on the endangered species list is a product of intradenominational relationships. In at least eight or ten of the larger Protestant denominations, there is a widening gap between local church leaders, both laity and clergy, and the national denominational headquarters. One evidence of this is the recent rapid increase in the number of supporters in the caucuses that come out publicly in opposition to the stance of the national denominational leadership.

In the 1950s and 1960s these tended to be caucuses of liberal clergy and liberal laity who disagreed with the policies of what was perceived to be more conservative national leadership. In the 1990s the renewal caucuses are more likely to be protesting what they perceive to be excessively liberal national leadership.

Far more significant, however, than the location of the liberal and conservative factions is a change in language. In the 1950s and the 1960s, the local protesters *disagreed* with the *policies* of the national leadership. Today the word *disagree* has been replaced by the word *distrust*. The word *policies* has been replaced by the word *personnel*. It is far easier to live with disagreement on policies than it is to coexist with distrust of individuals.

A public parallel of this relationship between congregational leaders and national denominational leadership is the growing hostility expressed by air-traffic controllers toward the Federal Aviation Administration. Some are indifferent or detached, but many are ready to take down the whole structure.[6]

The key variable in this conflict is the role of the regional denominational judicatory (conference, convention, district, synod, classis, presbytery, diocese, region). A growing number are aggressively building partnerships with congregations around three goals: (a) strengthening congregational life, (b) developing new missions, and (c) resourcing congregational leaders. This tends to further isolate the national denominational agencies. A smaller, but significant, number of regional judicatories, often for financial reasons, have chosen to partner with national denominational agencies. This tends to isolate them from the renewal caucuses. A third group of regional judicatories have attempted to find space to sit on the fence, but what once was a rail fence has been replaced by barbed wire.

This growing level of distrust has complicated life for the executives and professional staff of the national denominational agencies. This can be illustrated by the huge array of responses to the situation.

The most common response, of course, is denial.

The second most common is, "All would be well if you would send us more money."

The third is to appoint a restructure committee.

A fourth is to increase the volume of mail from national agencies to regional judicatories and congregations.

A fifth is to ask the annual (or biennial or triennial or quadrennial) national denominational convention to adopt legislation that would further antagonize the local and/or regional leaders.

A sixth is to schedule regional "hearings" to enable local leaders to speak directly to national leaders in hopes of "clearing the air."

A seventh is to schedule huge regional and/or national inspirational rallies designed with the hope of recreating the denominational loyalties adults born at the turn of the century expressed toward their denominational leaders back in the 1950s. These tend to produce disappointingly small crowds because so many of the loyal denominationalists born in the 1875–1935 era are unable to attend.

An eighth response is to schedule a denomination-wide capital funds campaign for missions.

A ninth is to reduce staff and program expenditures to the level of anticipated income.

A tenth is for the new chief executive officer of that national denominational agency to decide (a) "We have two top priorities. One is to resource congregations to help them do their ministry more effectively, and the other is to resource our regional judicatories to help them fulfill their role," and (b) "I personally will accept the responsibility to re-earn the trust of our constituents and to rebuild our credibility with both congregational and regional leaders."

Which scenario is being followed in your denomination?

An eighth reason for questioning the future of denominational systems is the gradual recognition that organizing around the promotion of social justice is completely unlike creating a single-issue movement. Movements prosper when they can focus on a single issue. By contrast, the four contemporary major definitions of justice (libertarian, socialist, perfectionist, and welfare liberalism) are mutually incompatible and highly divisive.[7]

Another threat is the growing number of senior ministers, program directors, pastors, church musicians, worship leaders, and other program staff members of congregations who find their participation in the gatherings of their ad hoc network to be far more rewarding and enjoyable than attending a denominational meeting.

The biggest threat, however, may be whether that old unifying organizing principle of rallying congregations and church members together in support of the cause of world missions can be replaced by another equally powerful, unifying, and attractive cause.

One more example of the impact of change on denominational systems is the result of the large regional church emerging as the successor to the old neighborhood congregation. This has forced denominational officials responsible for new church development to choose from among several strategies. One is to seek to perpetuate the 1950s model that defined the constituency to be served by their place of residence, provide substantial long-term financial subsidies for those new missions, watch in frustration as one-third plateau with fewer than a hundred at worship and another third close, and blame the disappointments on the contemporary shortage of competent mission-developer pastors.

A second alternative is to define the constituency to be served by characteristics other than place of residence (Mandarin Chinese; Caribbean-born blacks; young, never-married American-born Anglos; adult children of Korean-born immigrants; people born in the 1956–68 era who are now on a serious self-identified religious quest; refugees from the Midwest now living in a retirement community in the Sunbelt; parents of very young children; recent immigrants from India; couples in an intercultural marriage; and so on), recruit a mission-developer pastor who displays the same characteristics, and launch a new mission in rented or leased facilities.

A third is to create a partnership that includes that regional judicatory plus leaders from three very large regional congregations, enlist the three- to seven-person team required to build a large new regional church, use those three congregations as the training base to socialize that newly created team in the way to be a large church in that part of the world, and launch that new mission.

A fourth is to encourage a long-established congregation that meets in an obsolete building on an inadequate site at a poor location to relocate and make a fresh start in the new millennium.

A fifth is to persuade a mission-minded large congregation to accept the central responsibility for planting a new mission.

A sixth is to convince the appropriate congregations that the time has come for them to become multisite churches.

A seventh is to search for and resource the entrepreneurial pastor who possesses the gifts required for an effective church planter.

An eighth alternative, and by far the most difficult to implement, is to concentrate available denominational resources on "redeveloping" those congregations with an aging and numerically shrinking membership. One reason this is difficult is because a far higher level of competence is required in the person asked to renew the old than is needed to create the new.

A ninth alternative is to redefine the role of the denominational agency or regional judicatory from "doing new church development" to "making it happen." This new role calls for the regional judicatory or the denominational agency to (a) challenge every congregation to be engaged in one expression or another of church planting, (b) build a list of alternative forms of engagement in that effort, (c) help each congregation choose the method the members feel competent and comfortable with, and (d) resource each congregation to enable it to design and implement an action plan.

The list of possibilities include (a) committing to three years of financial support to a specific new mission, (b) sending volunteers to help a new mission construct a meeting place, (c) enlisting a team of volunteers to be trained to be part of the team that will start a new mission, (d) encouraging midsized congregations to use "a church-within-a-church" strategy to reach a different slice of the population, (e) creating a coalition of three or four congregations that would plant a new mission, (f) becoming a two-site congregation, (g) creating two or three or four or five or six off-campus faith communities staffed by volunteers every year, (h) encouraging large congregations to create a staff position that would be filled by a minister who would be trained to leave after a year or two (and be replaced by another trainee) to be the team leader for a three- to seven-person team who would plant a new big church, or (i) serving as the incubator for a new ethnic minority mission.

A tenth alternative is to deny there is a need to plant new missions to reach recent immigrants and new generations. Let the independent churches and the new denominations fill that vacuum if it really does exist.

One of the most highly visible consequences of the discontinuity with the past is the amount of land required for a new mission or for a congregation planning to relocate its meeting place. Most denominational officials of the 1950s regarded the recommendation of three acres offered by city planners as somewhere between excessive and extravagant. By the 1960s the standard recommendation was three to five acres. In the 1970s it was seven to ten. In the 1980s it was ten to fifteen acres. While exceptions could be justified on the basis of land costs or prize locations or the restrictions by local municipal land-use regulations, the 1990s saw an increasing number of congregations choosing sites that ranged between thirty and four hundred acres, and eighty acres was not uncommon.

What is a safe recommendation for the twenty-first century? About three times what the most optimistic person on the committee recommended.

Finally, which denominational systems are most likely to thrive in the twenty-first century?[8] One beginning point to respond to that question could be to reflect on six overlapping fork-in-the-road questions.

1. Those that are organized on the assumption that local (congregational and regional judicatory) leaders cannot be

trusted to make wise decisions or those that are organized on the basis of a high trust level of local leadership?

2. Those denominational systems that are designed primarily as regulatory bodies or those that are designed to function as creative resourcing agencies to work with congregational leaders in inventing new ministries to reach and minister with new generations and new constituencies?

3. Those that assume a high priority for every congregation is to resource the national denominational system or those that assume the primary purpose of all denominational systems is to resource congregations, including the creation of new worshiping communities?

4. Those that assume their primary source of financial support will be from member congregations or those that assume their primary sources of financial support will be individual donors, fees for services, income from investments, bequests, family foundations, and designated contributions by congregations?

5. Those that are organized with a hierarchical structure or those that are organized to function in a collegial or partner relationship with congregations?

6. Those that are organized and function around the law or those that reflect God's grace?

Which alternatives will most likely be a source of hope as you reflect on the future of your denominational system?

A Theological School Perspective

The consequences of the discontinuity with the past are having a tremendous impact all across American Christianity. The most severe impact may be in the Roman Catholic Church in America. What was once largely a network of immigrant churches and the source of great alarm among many Protestants might be seen to be evolving into a network of farm clubs feeding younger Christians into evangelical Protestant congregations.

From an institutional perspective, the second most threatened slice of the American Christian scene includes those denominational systems that expect congregations to (a) resource the denomination and (b) provide employment opportunities for fully credentialed clergy.

Close behind and tied for third place are two sets of institutions confronted with increasing discontinuity with the past. One is the middle-sized congregation averaging between 100 and 350 at worship (in some communities that second number may be as high as 700). The other is the twentieth-century model of a residential theological school. Whether both should be placed on the endangered species list is open to debate, but that may be the safe assumption in planning for their future.

This can be illustrated by looking at various facets of this discontinuity with the past in theological education—and this means another list!

1. While it is far from a universal concern, perhaps the most widely discussed problem is the inability of theological schools to attract substantial numbers of "the best and brightest" from among the people now in their early and midtwenties.

One result is an increasing competition among the schools for promising students. Forty years ago it was relatively rare for a theological school to have a full-time recruiter on the payroll. Today that is a widespread practice.

2. The most obvious is cost. Like other institutions of higher education, theological schools are beginning to price themselves out of the market. Student loans have become a financial trap, not a solution.

3. The mantra of the 1950s that a seminary should be "ecumenical, urban, and university-related" has turned out

to be a way to blur the distinctive identity and role of a particular school. If all schools are equal and all education should be ecumenical, why not choose a seminary closest to the student's place of residence or place of employment?[9]

Perhaps the biggest single step in the direction of erasing the denominational role of a theological school came in the summer of 1997 when five denominations—the Episcopal Church, the Presbyterian Church (U.S.A.), the United Church of Christ, the Reformed Church in America, and the Evangelical Lutheran Church in America—agreed that ecumenism was more important than perpetuating distinctive denominational belief systems or distinctive denominational traditions.

4. Distance learning is replacing residence-based education. For many students it is economically more attractive to live at home, perhaps continue in the present job, and commute a short distance to a classroom. Increasingly that classroom is in a church building, not on a seminary campus.

5. The increase in the number of "second career" adults enrolling in seminary changes the agenda they bring to the process. They express a need for professional training, not a graduate school degree.

Back when entrance into adulthood was one's twenty-first birthday, "going off to school" was part of the process of becoming an adult, and entering seminary at age 21 or 22 or 23 paralleled going to graduate school. The typical 41-year-old seminarian wants professional training, not more preparation for adulthood or academic training.

6. Overlapping that is the growing demand by seminary students to be taught by effective practitioners of ministry, rather than by academic scholars and researchers.

7. Perhaps the subtle point of discontinuity is the change in what should be transmitted. A primary reason for the emergence of that huge number of denominational seminaries in the 1840–1960 era was the felt need to transmit to

future generations of parish pastors "our belief system, our denominational culture, our denominational traditions, our value system, and our polity."

Three points of discontinuity with those nineteenth-century hopes have undermined that role. The first was the academic relocation from Jerusalem to Athens, from the city of faith to the city of knowledge, from a role as a professional school to a self-identified role as a graduate school that had to be consistent with the academic culture of a graduate school. Scholars replace practitioners in the effort to build a "great faculty."

The second was the ecumenical movement of the second half of the twentieth century. The new emphasis was to be on what we as Christians have in common, not on what distinguishes one Christian tradition from other traditions.

The third was the redefinition of "our constituency" from students coming from a particular denominational tradition to students living within two hundred to three hundred miles of our campus. The regional role moved ahead of denominational identity.

8. From this observer's perspective the most significant, and the most widely overlooked, point of discontinuity came out of the marketplace. What do the people who are going to employ the graduates want?

The old answer was that the congregations want someone who has internalized the distinctive belief system, the polity, the traditions, and the culture of their denomination. Theological schools were expected to do that, although by 1950 many were questioning whether that was a realistic expectation.

The policymakers in that growing number of megachurches today are looking for paid staff members, both lay and ordained, who understand the distinctive culture of the very large church in general; who fully understand and are completely supportive of the belief system, the culture, the polity, and the local traditions of this particular congregation; and, most important, who are persons of good character.

It is completely unrealistic to expect a theological school to produce the graduates who can meet that set of expectations. The most effective way to produce staff members who can meet those criteria is to focus on a select group of the members of that very large congregation and encourage them in their personal religious pilgrimage to consider the possibility of joining the staff of that congregation. The need for clearly defined academic preparation can be met by courses held in classrooms in that congregation's building or by commuting to a nearby classroom.

The key variable is that their learning experiences socialize them into the distinctive culture of that congregation, not into the academic culture of a graduate school.

The theological school with three or four or five dozen M. Div. degree candidates in each year's graduating class may be able to prepare students for the culture of the small or mid-sized congregation, but it is unrealistic to expect that school to prepare people for ministry in the very large churches.[10]

9. A few readers may argue that the most significant point of discontinuity with the past for this discussion is a product of the rise of American evangelicalism. Most, but not all, of the theological schools in the United States reflect a western European religious heritage and a western European approach to formal education. That is symbolized today by the head. By contrast, American evangelicalism is symbolized by the heart. The first focuses on God the Creator and the nouns and pronouns that should be used in referring to God. The second focuses on Christ the Savior and on words used to describe one's relationship to Jesus.[11]

10. Another burden placed on the theological school by the marketplace reflects a change in expectations. Up through the 1950s seminaries were expected to produce four kinds of generalists—pastors, missionaries, Christian educators, and musicians.

The large churches today want highly skilled specialists,

including ministers of missions; experts in the intellectual, social, and emotional development of children, from birth to age three; parish nurses; worship leaders; experts in visual communication; writers; executive pastors; experts in ministries with young adults; ministers of recreation; and dozens of other specialists.

11. From a bureaucratic and professional perspective, a major point of discontinuity and tension is in the accreditation system. The problems include the criteria for accreditation, the autonomy of the schools, the proliferation of accrediting bodies, the use of standards that may be appropriate for a secular institution but are incompatible with the culture and goals of a Christian school, and the credibility of the whole system.

12. Several veteran seminary teachers point to the agendas the students bring as the source of great discontinuity. As recently as the 1950s a reasonably safe assumption was that every first-year student already was a deeply committed Christian coming to prepare for a full-time Christian vocation. Today many adults on a self-identified spiritual or vocational quest see the seminary as a place to help them on that pilgrimage. Others come believing the seminary should be and is a therapy center. A third group come to investigate whether the Christian faith is what they seek.

While this is not offered as an exhaustive list, it does illustrate the point that theological schools are experiencing the consequences of the discontinuity with the past that is the central theme of this book.

The future of theological education is of such crucial importance that it may justify chopping down one more tree to look at this issue from another perspective.

What is the primary purpose of a theological school? What is the number one reason for its existence?

The more precisely, the more clearly, and the more narrowly this question can be answered, the easier it will be for the administration and the trustees to allocate scarce resources among competing demands. The aging of any institution, either religious or secular, usually is accompanied by what some describe as "mission creep." The original mission was stated in one brief sentence; a few generations later a paragraph is required. Eventually that paragraph grows into a long list of missions, purposes, and goals, many of which are mutually incompatible. This "diffusion of purpose" has many predictable consequences, including long committee meetings, quarrels over the priorities in the allocation of scarce resources, capital funds campaigns, short-tenured chief executive officers, intensive and expensive efforts to attract and serve new constituencies, the resignation and departure of several valuable players, a blurred identity, and the erosion of loyalty among the constituents.

Normal institutional pressures make it easy to expand that growing list of central goals and difficult to reduce it. If that lengthening mission statement can be reduced to two or three internally consistent and institutionally compatible goals, the administrative task becomes possible. When that list of goals grows into a two-digit number, the search for unanimity often leads to the lowest common denominator.

Why do we exist as a theological school? What is our primary purpose as a theological school?

1. To prepare candidates for ordination in our denominational tradition.

2. To prepare persons who feel called by God to serve as parish pastors for that vocation, in our denominational tradition.

One consequence of discontinuity is that in 1890 these two statements might have had a 90 percent overlap. Today that overlap is no more than 30 percent.

3. To transmit to all students the distinctive doctrines, belief systems, polity traditions, and culture of our expression of the Christian faith.

4. To serve as a regional, intercultural, and interdenominational theological school that focuses on preparing students for the parish ministry. We assume that their denominational culture, polity, belief systems, and traditions will be instilled in them by their denominational system.

5. To prepare students who feel called to teach in a theological school for that vocation.

6. To provide relevant and meaningful learning experiences in a predominantly African American environment for American-born, African-born, and Caribbean-born blacks who have been called by God to the Christian ministry and to equip them for that vocation.

7. To provide relevant and meaningful learning experiences in a predominantly western European educational environment for persons of an ethnic minority background who have been called by God to the Christian ministry in an Anglo culture and to equip them for that vocation.

8. To serve as a therapy center for troubled adults with serious personal, psychological, and emotional problems.

9. To serve as a spiritual retreat center for adults who may not be contemplating entering a full-time professional Christian vocation but who seek help to be able to move into the next stage of their personal, spiritual, and vocational pilgrimage.

10. To help self-identified Christian believers discover their vocation.

11. To help persons on a personal religious quest discover whether or not the Christian faith is for them.

12. To provide secure employment for tenured faculty who are too young to retire but who cannot find other satisfactory employment.

13. To equip adults who have been called by God to the vocation of church planter to be able to plant new missions that will be self-governing, self-financing, self-expressing, and self-propagating within twelve months following their first public worship service.

14. To equip self-identified church planters to go create megachurches that will be averaging at least seven hundred in worship by their seventh anniversary.

15. To equip adults for specialized staff positions such as minister of health, minister of missions, minister of prayer, executive pastor, director of ministries with families that include teenagers, pastoral counselor, minister of preaching, facilitator of small groups, coordinator of volunteers, director of ministries with families that include children from newborn to age three, worship team leader, minister of evangelism, minister of recreation, and media specialist.

16. To offer meaningful and relevant continuing-education experiences for both clergy and laity in all sizes and types of congregations.

17. To train recent immigrants to the United States to serve as pastors of predominantly Anglo congregations.

18. To serve as a research and development center for our denomination.

19. To provide short-term equipping experiences to prepare lay volunteers to serve on congregational ministry teams.

20. To raise enough money from individual donors and other sources to financially subsidize most of the above.

Policy makers in theological education are responding in various ways to these changes and demands. The most predictable, of course, is to focus on raising more money as insurance against the future. Another is to build new residential housing on the campus, including more housing for married students with children, in the hope that this will guarantee a residence-based constituency paralleling the 1950s. A third is to decentralize with extension centers in several locations. A fourth is illustrated by Dallas Theological Seminary and Fuller Theological Seminary. That is to carve out a distinctive niche as an international and nondenominational school. A fifth is to work harder at encouraging churches to send students to "our school." A sixth is to emphasize the Doctor of Ministry program. A seventh is to merge with another school. An eighth is to expand the course offerings to become a graduate school of religion, social work, counseling, and administration. A ninth is to look for a new president who will be an effective fund-raiser. A tenth is to build a partnership with one or two or three megachurches and move a chunk of the learning experiences for students to the megachurch. An eleventh is to ask the denomination for increased financial support. A twelfth is to concentrate on preparing students to serve as bivocational pastors of small to midsized congregations.

And that, again, is far from a complete list. It is, however, one way to end a book on the theme that discontinuity with the past does produce consequences in the future.

What Next?

Finally, how do you respond to this discussion of some of the probable consequences to this discontinuity in the context of ministry in America? With hope? Or with despair? With eagerness to see what the future will bring? Or with gratitude that you are only a few years from retirement? Or with regret that you may not live long enough to experience ministry throughout the first half of the twenty-first century? Your answer probably will be determined by whether today you see yourself living under the threat of change or looking forward eagerly in the hope of change.

This observer is willing to speculate briefly on a perspective from the year 2050.

First, none of the leaders of that day will bring firsthand memories of how it was back in the 1950s or 1960s into the discussions on designing a strategy for the second half of the twenty-first century. For at least a few readers, that may be the best news in this book!

Second, the proportion of churchgoers in American Christianity who are deeply committed disciples and apostles probably will be at least double or triple the proportions of 1999, while the proportion who are "lukewarm"[12] in their faith will shrink dramatically.

Third, the proportion of Protestant congregations that accept the role as "Kingdom-building churches" will at least quadruple, while the proportion that are driven by institutional survival goals will drop by at least one-half. That will be accompanied by an increase in the proportion that are implementing effective strategies for "congregation building."[13]

Fourth, the traditional system of congregations relying on denominational structures as the basis for relating to other churches gradually will continue to fade away. The replacement system will be networks of like-minded congregations working together in ministry and mission. Some of these will be intradenominational networks working across judicatory boundaries. Others will be nondenominational or interdenominational networks.

Fifth, the number one social action cause of American Christians in the nineteenth century led to the Thirteenth, Fourteenth, and Fifteenth Amendments to the United States Constitution. The number one cause for the twentieth century was the Civil Rights movement. The number one cause for the first half of the twenty-first century will be the efforts of the Christian churches to make this a better world for children.

Sixth, for many individual Christians the most significant consequence will be the impact of the continued expansion of the ministry of the laity on their personal and spiritual journey.

From this observer's perspective, that represents a foundation to be optimistic about what the twenty-first century will bring.

How do you view it?

NOTES

―❦―

Introduction

1. In a wonderful book, the late Dr. Lewis Thomas recalls that as recently as the early 1930s the responsibilities of a physician were modest—diagnosis, explanation, prognosis, and reassurance. The practice of medicine was relatively simple. Then came sulfanilamide and eventually hundreds of new miracle drugs. The practice of medicine became vastly more demanding, complicated, challenging—and satisfying. Instead of simply describing the probable course that particular illnesses normally followed, physicians now actually could cure illnesses. Lewis Thomas, *The Youngest Science* (New York: Viking Penguin, 1983), pp. 28-35.

A parallel is that the role of the pastor has evolved from the caring shepherd to the leader who helps to transform believers into disciples and apostles by challenging them to become what God intended them to be and to grow beyond self-imposed ceilings. That is a more challenging and a more difficult assignment than feeding and caring for the sheep, but it also can be a more satisfying role!

1. Continuity to Discontinuity

1. A leading contemporary philosopher commented on this trend in these words, "One of the most fascinating—and terrifying—features of the era in which I write this is the steady erosion of acceptance of large institutional structures round the world." John R. Searle, *The Construction of Social Reality* (New York: Free Press, 1995), p. 117.

2. The definition of the road to salvation is now being used as a line of demarcation in classifying theological schools. See Jackson W. Carroll et al., *Being There* (New York: Oxford University Press, 1997), p. 204. Also see Dennis L. Okholm and Timothy R. Phillips, eds., *More Than One Way? Four Views on Salvation in a Pluralistic World* (Grand Rapids, Mich.: Zondervan, 1997).

3. This is described briefly in Lyle E. Schaller, *Tattered Trust* (Nashville: Abingdon Press, 1996), pp. 49-51 and in far more detail with a narrower focus in Paul K. Conkin, *American Originals* (Chapel Hill: University of North Carolina Press, 1997). For a description of the emergence of three new "Made in America" religious movements, see Donald E. Miller, *Reinventing American Protestantism: Christianity in the New Millennium* (Berkeley: University of California Press, 1997).

4. Conkin, *American Originals,* pp. 277-93.

5. A comment by Jim Muertha quoted by Howard Reich and Melita Marie Garza, "Even Before Solti's Death His Music Has Been Dying," *The Chicago Tribune* (September 10, 1997), pp. 1 and 20.

6. For reflections on the recent history of interchurch cooperation, see Lyle E. Schaller, *The Small Membership Church* (Nashville: Abingdon Press, 1994), pp. 59-77.

7. See David B. McCarthy, "The Emerging Importance of Presbyterian Polity," *The Organizational Revolution: Presbyterians and American Denominationalism,* ed. John M. Mulder et al. (Louisville: Westminster John Knox Press, 1992), pp. 279-306.

8. Lyle E. Schaller, *44 Ways to Revitalize the Women's Organization* (Nashville: Abingdon Press, 1990), pp. 19-47.

2. The Big Seven

1. Thomas W. Hanchett, "U. S. Tax Policy and the Shopping Center Boom of the 1950s and 1960s," *The American Historical Review* (October 1996), p. 1098.

2. Stephen E. Ambrose, *Eisenhower: The President* (New York: Simon & Schuster, 1984), pp. 547-48.

3. Bob Greene, "The Secret Was in the Combination of Big and Small," *Chicago Tribune,* July 23, 1997.

4. The statistics on the sales of groceries are based on data gathered by the Economic Research Service of the U. S. Department of Agriculture and published annually in *The Statistical Abstract of the United States.*

5. A revealing history of American Christianity that lifts up the winners and losers concept is Roger Finke and Rodney Stark, *The Churching of America, 1776–1990* (New Brunswick, N.J.: Rutgers University Press, 1992).

6. For an analysis of the changing foundations of social networks, see Peter F. Drucker, "The Age of Social Transformation," *The Atlantic Monthly* (November 1994).

3. New Generations Bring a New Context

1. John T. McGreevy, "Thinking on One's Own: Catholicism in the American Intellectual Imagination, 1928–1960," *The Journal of American History* (June 1997), pp. 97-131.

2. David K. Shipler, *A Country of Strangers* (New York: Alfred A. Knopf, 1997).

3. A fascinating account of the stress created in the churches by the Civil Rights movement of the 1960s is Charles Marsh, *God's Long Summer* (Princeton, N.J.: Princeton University Press, 1997).

4. Two outstanding books on the subject of teams are Warren G. Bennis and Patricia Ward Biederman, *Organizing Genius* (Reading, Mass.: Addison-Wesley Publishing Co., 1997) and James C. Collins and Jerry I. Porras, *Built to Last* (New York: HarperCollins, 1997). A challenging, but supportive, essay is, "The Myth of the Top Management Team," *Harvard Business Review* (November/December 1997), pp. 83-91.

5. Quoted in Stephanie Coontz, *The Way We Really Are* (New York: Basic Books, 1997).

6. Michael S. Resnick et al., "Protecting Adolescents from Harm," *Journal of the Medical Association,* vol. 278, no. 10 (September 10, 1997), pp. 823-33.

Notes

7. Leon R. Kass, "The End of Courtship," *The Public Interest* (Winter 1997), pp. 39-63.

8. For a brief introduction to two sides of the debate on marriage, see the series of essays under the umbrella title, "Family Feud" in *The American Prospect* (May/June 1997, July/August 1997, and September/October 1997).

9. *Course & Professor Evaluations* (Berkeley: Associated Students University of California Academic Affairs Office, 1997).

10. Ken Auletta, "The Microsoft Provocateur," *The New Yorker* (May 12, 1997), pp. 66-72.

11. For a superb analysis of the growing emphasis on entertainment, see William D. Romanowski, *Pop Culture Wars: Religion and the Role of Entertainment in American Life* (Downers Grove, Ill.: InterVarsity, 1997). An earlier and provocative analysis was Neil Postman, *Amusing Ourselves to Death* (New York: Penguin Books, 1985). One critic argues that instead of adults socializing youth into the culture, teenagers are now socializing adults into an entertainment-driven culture. Michiko Katutani, "Adolescence Rules!" *The New York Times* (May 11, 1997).

12. One critic claims money and greed are the villains. See Norman Lebrecht, *Who Killed Classical Music?* (Secaucus, N.J.: Birch Lane Press/Carol Publishing Group, 1997).

13. William Glasser, *The Identity Society* (New York: Harper & Row, 1972).

14. Lyle E. Schaller, *Community Organization: Conflict and Reconciliation* (Nashville: Abingdon Press, 1966), pp. 49-114.

15. McGreevy, "Thinking on One's Own."

16. Younger readers who never experienced the anti-Catholicism of the pre-1960s may want to read the biography of one of the leading liberal Methodist bishops of that era. Robert Moats Miller, *Bishop G. Bromley Oxnam* (Nashville: Abingdon Press, 1990).

17. It is not irrelevant to note the title of a popular history of American Methodism, Charles W. Ferguson, *Organized to Beat the Devil* (Garden City, N.Y.: Doubleday & Co., 1954).

18. For an up-to-date history of the Roman Catholic Church in the United States, see Charles R. Morris, *American Catholic* (New York: Random House, 1997).

19. For a readable introduction to how the brain develops in babies, see Ronald Kotulak, *Inside the Brain* (Kansas City, Mo.: Andrews McMeel, 1996). For a scholarly account, see Stanley I. Greenspan, *The Growth of the Mind: And the Endangered Origins of Intelligence* (Reading, Mass.: Addison-Wesley Publishing Co., 1996). For an introduction to the importance of music in early childhood development, see Paul Madaula, "Music: An Invitation to Listening, Language and Learning," *Early Childhood Connections* (Spring 1997), pp. 32-35.

20. An exceptionally useful introduction to the American welfare state is Theda Skocpol, *Protecting Soldiers and Mothers* (Cambridge, Mass.: Harvard University Press, 1992).

21. For a friendly, but critical, appraisal of the impact of the bureaucratization of tax-supported human services, see Andrew J. Polsky, *The Rise of the Therapeutic State* (Princeton, N.J.: Princeton University Press, 1991), pp. 178-224.

22. Susan Baur, *The Intimate Hour* (Boston: Houghton Mifflin Co., 1997).

4. Seven Neglected Changes

1. For a fascinating introduction to the world of collecting experiences, see Esther Dyson, *Release 2.0* (New York: Broadway Books, 1997).

Notes

2. James Turner, *Without God, With Creed: The Origins of Unbelief in America* (Baltimore: The Johns Hopkins University Press, 1985).

3. Ibid., p. 199.

4. Ibid., p. 171.

5. This point also is made by George M. Marsden, *The Soul of the American University: From Protestant Establishment to Established Non-Belief* (New York: Oxford University Press, 1994).

6. Ibid., pp. 108-70.

7. Ibid., pp. 240-48. See also Conrad Cherry, *Hurrying Toward Zion* (Bloomington: Indiana University Press, 1995), pp. 1-24, 243-45.

8. W. Clark Gilpin, "The Theological Schools: Transmission, Transformation, and Transcendence of Denominational Culture," *Beyond Establishment*, ed. Jackson W. Carroll and Wade Clark Roof (Louisville: Westminster John Knox Press, 1993), pp. 188-204.

9. George M. Marsden, *The Outrageous Idea of Christian Scholarship* (New York: Oxford University Press, 1997). See also "Is There Also a Place for Theology in Academia?" *Wilson Quarterly* (Spring 1997), pp. 130-31. For a brief, lucid, and revealing analysis of the changing role of Christian colleges, see Robert Wood Lynn, "The Survival of Recognizably Protestant Colleges: Reflections on Old-Line Protestantism," *The Secularization of the Academy*, ed. George M. Marsden and Bradley J. Longfield (New York: Oxford University Press, 1992), pp. 170-74.

10. Marsden, *The Soul of the American University*, pp. 281-90.

11. This story is retold in the videotape, *Trial of Hope*, narrated by Hal Holbrook and produced by Groberg Communications, Bountiful, Utah.

12. Arthur Levine, "The Making of a Generation," *Change* (September/October 1993), pp. 8-15.

13. For a more extensive discussion of this strategy by two of its pioneers, see J. Timothy Ahlen and J. V. Thomas, *The Key Church Strategy: One Church—Many Congregations* (Nashville: Abingdon Press, 1998).

5. What Are the Consequences?

1. A brief review of the differences between denominationally affiliated congregations and independent churches is offered in Lyle E. Schaller, *Tattered Trust* (Nashville: Abingdon Press, 1996), pp. 31-33.

2. See Lyle E. Schaller, *The Small Membership Church* (Nashville: Abingdon Press, 1994), pp. 23-39.

3. Mark Starr, "Touching all Bases," *Newsweek* (March 10, 1997), p. 77.

4. Potential questions to be asked can be found in Lyle E. Schaller, *The Interventionist* (Nashville: Abingdon Press, 1997).

5. This point is made very forcefully in an analysis of the hiring procedures of universities by Cary Nelson, "The Real Problem with Tenure Is Incompetent Faculty Hiring," *The Chronicle of Higher Education* (November 14, 1997), pp. 34-35.

6. For a pilot's perspective on the relationship of the air-traffic controllers and the Federal Aviation Administration, see William Langewiesche, "Slam and Jam," *The Atlantic Monthly* (October 1997), pp. 87-100. The author writes, "Among the controllers, the feeling of abandonment is so strong . . . that some controllers would be willing to take the entire structure down." This observer's perception is that a growing number of pastors feel the same way about their national denominational structure.

Notes

7. For an analysis of incompatible definitions of justice, see James P. Sterba, "Recent Work on Alternative Conceptions of Justice," *American Philosophical Quarterly*, vol. 23 (January 1986), pp. 1-22.

8. Three Presbyterian scholars offered a two-sentence answer to this question about the future of denominations, "By the 1990s, the outline of the denominational revolution was clear. Congregations, rather than denominations, had become the primary mission organizations in American mainstream Protestantism." Milton J. Coalter, John M. Mueller, and Louis B. Weeks, *Vital Signs* (Grand Rapids, Mich.: William B. Eerdmans Publishing Co., 1996), p. 99.

9. Two provocative accounts of the huge range of approaches to theological education are Conrad Cherry, *Hurrying Toward Zion* (Bloomington: Indiana University Press, 1995) and Jackson W. Carroll et al., *Being There* (New York: Oxford University Press, 1997).

10. This question as to whether it is reasonable or fair to expect divinity schools to train people for ministry in large congregations is discussed by Ronald E. Miller, *Reinventing American Protestantism: Christianity in the New Millennium* (Berkeley: University of California Press, 1997), pp. 166 and 188.

11. This contrast between two varieties of contemporary theological schools comes through with remarkable clarity in Carroll, *Being There*.

12. This category of "lukewarmness" is borrowed from John B. Cobb, Jr., *Reclaiming the Church: Where the Mainline Church Went Wrong and What to Do About It* (Louisville: Westminster John Knox Press, 1997).

13. The distinction between a "congregation-building" approach to ministry and a "Kingdom-building" approach can be found in Lyle E. Schaller, *44 Questions for Congregational Self-Appraisal* (Nashville: Abingdon Press, 1998), pp. 44-48.